Information Support for The Legal Profession

INFORMATION SUPPORT FOR THE LEGAL PROFESSION

Justice Gopal Sri Ram
Judge
Court of Appeal
Kuala Lumpur
Malaysia

Published By:

Ess Ess Publications

For

Sarada Ranganathan Endowment for
Library Science
Bangalore

Published by:
Ess Ess Publications
4837/24, Ansari Road,
Darya Ganj,
New Delhi-110 002.
Tel.: 23260807, 41563444
Fax: 41563334
E-mail: info@essessreference.com
www.essessreference.com

For:
Sarada Ranganathan Endowment for Library Science
702, 'Upstairs', 42nd Cross, III Block,
Rajajinagar,
Bangalore-560 010.
Tel. : 080-23305109
E-mail: srels@dataone.in

Rs.325/-

First Published - 2008

ISBN: 81-7000-536-1 (10 Digit)
978-81-7000-536-0 (13 Digit)

Printed at Salasar Imaging Systems

PRINTED IN INDIA

Dr. S.R. Ranganathan Memorial Lecture Series, 14 (2006)

INFORMATION SUPPORT FOR THE LEGAL PROFESSION

Ranganathan's Five Laws of Library Science

Books are for Use
Every Reader his/her Book
Every Book its Reader
Save the Time of the Reader
Library is a Growing Organism

Contents

PREFACE

The Sarada Ranganathan Endowment for Library Science, Bangalore, has instituted Dr. S.R. Ranganathan Memorial Lectures for inviting eminent specialists for delivering lectures in special areas. Justice Gopal Sri Ram, Judge, Court of Appeal, Kuala Lumpur, Malaysia, graciously accepted our invitation and delivered three lectures on "Information Support for the Legal Profession" at Bangalore in 2006. His lectures are reproduced in this publication.

The first lecture deals with the why of information support. It is needed for citing precedents. The role and value of precedent in law are explained. Precedent is a judge-made law. Next to legislative enactments, decisions of courts form most important sources of law. Interpretations of statutes (Acts of Parliament) by a judge is a judge-made law. The doctrine of binding precedent is explained. The system of courts is hierarchical. Decisions of higher courts are binding on lower courts. A disadvantage of precedent is that it locks one to a decision which produces injustice. Actual cases are given for each type of precedents. The practices followed in various courts in India, Britain, Malaysia and other commonwealth countries are explained. At the end, two examples are given illustrating how the stranglehold of strict adherence to precedents leads to injustice. The practice of citing precedents calls for information support for the legal profession.

The second lecture describes the historical development of courts in England, India, Malaysia, etc., and the records developed by them for reporting cases. The various types of records generated starting from the rolls of the Court (1220s), Year-Books (1250), English Reports, Law Reports, etc., and their use for citing precedents are explained giving examples. The system of law reporting in India from 1774 and the documents generated are described. The role of the Incorporated Council of Law Reporting for England and Wales (ICLR) with the main objective of publishing Law Reports of judicial decisions of the Superior and Appellate Courts in England, at a moderate price, and its features are given. A short account is given of law reporting in Malaysia. Appendix 1 gives some examples of cases where binding precedents do not provide a just result when it should.

The third lecture deals with information support for legal research. The primary source of information for practitioners and judges continues to be text books. Examples of personal experience in tracking information for various cases step by step are given as illustrations. The problems of access to information are discussed. The volume of legal publications are rapidly increasing. The pressure on storage space, increasing cost of publications, documents in CD-ROM formats, online digital databases and services available are some of the issues discussed. The emergence of legal information institutes in various countries and their initiatives for providing free access to legal information are moves in the right direction.

If everyone concerned in the justice process are fully armed with all relevant authorities, the chances for arriving at a just decision are better. Appendix 2 deals with academic writings that influenced decisions, citing examples.

The topic of "Information Support for the Legal Profession" is presented by the author in a pleasant, lucid, and interesting manner. Coming from an erudite scholar, a leading lawyer and an experienced judge, the book has weight. It provides interesting reading. It is a useful publication for law students, practitioners, judges, research workers, and the general public.

S. Parthasarathy

Member, SRELS

Chennai

30 Jan. 2008

Foreword

Information support is of great importance in every professional field and work. It is, *inter alia*, important to the legal profession. The law is enduring. It serves the society and serves the exigencies of change of times and social needs. The principles of basic law are eternal and universal. But concepts change from time to time according to the needs of the society and the demand of public interest. A person in the legal profession has to keep abreast with development of law. Information plays a key role in this regard. The law changes and develops not merely by legislation but by the disciplined interpretative skill of judges. While judges follow the principle of binding precedents, they shape the law to the needs of the situation by appropriately interpreting such precedents. In this process, they make law to meet the ends of justice so that law and justice are congruous.

The lectures of Hon'ble Mr. Justice Gopal Sriram, Judge, Court of Appeal, Malaysia are instructive, interesting and thought provoking. It is so thoughtful of Sarada Ranganathan Endowment for Library Science, Bangalore to come forward to publish his lectures under the title 'Information support for the legal profession'. I commend the book particularly to those who have thirst for knowledge and have the habit of reading books. The book will be a useful addition to libraries.

K. PARASARAN
Former Attorney General for India

About Sarada Ranganathan Endowment for Library Science

The Sarada Ranganathan Endowment for Library Science (SRELS), founded by Dr. S.R. Ranganathan in 1961, is registered as a Charitable Endowment with the Government of India (1963).

The aims of the Endowment briefly are:

* To improve the library and information services in India
* To train library and information service personnel
* To promote the provision of efficient library and information service
* To apply research results to library and information studies

The objectives of the Endowment are:

* Furthering the cause of library and information service
* Organising Seminars and Workshops on recent

developments in library and information science and the related fields.

* Organising periodically courses of lectures on recent developments in library and information science and related fields by national and international experts

* Supporting the publication of these lectures and of other nascent ideas in the field of library and information science.

The Endowment is furthering these objectives by publishing a periodical entitled *SRELS Journal of Information Management* (*formerly, Library Science with a slant to Documentation* (from 1964 to 1988), and *Library Science with slant to Documentation and Information Studies* (from 1988 to 1999). Workshops, Lecture presentations and Seminars are also organized periodically.

There are three series of lectures organized under the auspices of the Endowment:

1. Sarada Ranganathan Endowment Lectures. (1965-);
2. Dr. S.R. Ranganathan Memorial Lectures. (1973-); and
3. Curzon Co-Seshachalam Endowment Lectures. (2001-).

The Endowment is thankful to Hon'ble Justice Gopal Sri Ram for delivering the 14th S.R. Ranganathan Memorial Lectures on Information Support for the Legal Profession on 23, 24, and 25 August 2006 at the Cannara Bank School of Management Studies, Bangalore.

The Endowment is also grateful to Sri. K. Parasaran, Senior Advocate and Former Attorney General for India, for writing the foreword for the book.

We are grateful to Prof. S. Parthasarathy for presiding over the lectures and for writing the preface for the book.

The Endowment is thankful to Prof. Dr. A. Jayagovind, Vice Chancellor, National Law School of India University, Bangalore for inaugurating the lectures on 23rd August 2006.

K.N. Prasad
Executive Officer
Sarada Ranganathan
Endowment for Library Science

Lecture 1

INFORMATION SUPPORT FOR THE LEGAL PROFESSION : THE ROLE AND VALUE OF PRECEDENT

1. INTRODUCTORY REMARKS

Why is information support of importance to all branches of the legal profession? The answer lies in two words: precedent and persuasion. I will deal with the first at some length later in this lecture. Let me for the present deal with the second.

The essence of a lawyer's skill is the power of persuasion. The task is to persuade his or her audience to agree with the particular view advanced through the power of argument, whether oral or written. The audience may be either a tribunal or a readership or the public at large. If you are a practising advocate, your audience is usually a court or other tribunal. If you are an academic, then your audience is the rest of the profession – the judges, the lawyers and other academics. And if you are a judge, then your audience is the world at large.

Knowledge is essential to be able to put forward

an argument. You cannot speak with authority and convince someone unless you have the requisite knowledge. And you cannot acquire knowledge without information. Hence, from the earliest of times, information support has played a vital role in the legal profession. Information in law is important not only in the advancement of litigation. It is also important to prevent useless litigation by convincing your client that he will be wasting his time and money in bringing or resisting an action. The alternative to an amicable settlement is as effective if not better as a case fought and won.

There is another aspect of information for practising lawyers that is often overlooked. It has to do with what lawyers call conveyancing. In its narrowest sense it refers to the process by which a person may transfer his immoveable property to another and to all those matters appurtenant to that process. But in today's world it refers to a whole gamut of things, from the preparation of a will or an agreement or charge documents of all sorts. It is important for the lawyer – acting as the draftsman of the particular document – to make sure that it reflects what the parties want in order to reduce the prospects of protracted and expensive litigation. A lawyer who drafts such documents can gain much assistance from other similar documents prepared on an earlier occasion. To help lawyers in this respect there are texts that produce examples of such documents. These earlier documents are also referred to by lawyers as precedents. But they have nothing whatsoever to do with the doctrine of precedent that I referred to earlier.

There is another reason why relevant information is vital to the lawyer. The result of a particular dispute is often, if not always, based on analogy. What the advocate tries to do is to demonstrate that his client's case is the same or very similar to another case already decided by the courts. He will argue that since the litigant in that other case succeeded, so should his client in the instant case. So, it is necessary to be able to find a case as close to the one now before the court. You cannot do that unless you have the information support to locate such a case. Usually, such support will come from a textbook on the particular subject. The textbook usually sets out the principle of general application and then provides individual cases to illustrate the application or non-application of that principle.

2. WHAT IS PRECEDENT?

Speaking in very general terms, "precedent" refers to an earlier decision by a court. Geoffrey Marshall of Oxford says this about "precedent":

> "The term 'precedent' itself has a number of applications. In the first place, it is sometimes applied without further thought or analysis to a body of allegedly relevant prior decisions (typically gathered together and cited by counsel on both sides in a common law case). Secondly, 'precedent' can be used as a description of the result or outcome of a particular decision that is thought to be of some significance. Thirdly, the term may be used to state a wider rule that the decision in a particular case is alleged to instantiate or illustrate.

> These three usages might be called the advocate's sense, the judge's sense and the scholar's or critic's sense".

Oliver J. explained the doctrine of binding precedent or *stare decisis* in ***Midland Bank v Hett, Stubbs & Kemp (a firm) [1979] Ch 384*** as follows:

> "I have been led by counsel through a bewildering complex of authorities many of which are not easy to reconcile with the principles established in subsequent cases in superior courts or, in some cases, with one another. The task of a judge of first instance faced with this situation is not an easy one. Our system of courts is hierarchical and he must on the one hand follow and apply those principles of law which have been clearly laid down by higher authority whilst, at the same time, avoiding the risk of abrogating to himself a function which properly belongs only to a higher tribunal and which he has no power to exercise even where reason might tempt him to do so. Even the principles which he should follow when confronted by apparently conflicting decisions of superior courts are not always clear and, where they are clear, they are not always easy to apply, for their application may itself depend on a disputable interpretation of a decision of a superior court.
>
> The principles so far as relevant to the present case appear to me to be these and I adopt them in my approach to counsel

for the plaintiffs' submissions. (1) A decision of the House of Lords resting on or establishing a general doctrine binds all inferior courts and represents the law of the land until it is altered by legislation or, nowadays, departed from by the house itself: see *Great Western Railway Co v Mostyn (Owners), The Mostyn* [1928] AC 57 at 82, *the Wilkinson (Taunton Revenue Officer) v Sibley and Donovan* [1932] 1 KB 194 at 200. (2) A decision of an inferior court may be treated as having been overruled by a decision of a superior court with which it is shown to be inconsistent, although it has not been expressly so stated by those who concur in such decision: see *Consett Industrial and Provident Society Ltd v Consett Iron Co Ltd* [1922] 2 Ch 135 at 173. (3) An interpretation of a statute or of a decision of the House of Lords by the Court of Appeal is binding on that court even if it subsequently regards the interpretation as erroneous: see *Williams v Glasbrook Brothers Ltd* [1947] 2 AIR ER 884 and *Miliangos v George Frank (Textiles) Ltd* [1976] AC 443 at 479. *A fortiori* such an interpretation binds an inferior court. (4) Where there are conflicting decisions of the Court of Appeal, that court is free to choose which it will follow: see *Young v Bristol Aeroplane Co Ltd* [1946] 1 All ER 98, [1946] AC 163. The position of a judge at first instance when faced with such a conflict is not clear.

He must, I think, equally be free to choose unless it is to be suggested that he must follow that decision which is latest in point of time".

To complete the picture it may be added that the House of Lords was until 1966 bound by its own decisions. In that year, the Lord Chancellor sitting with all the ten Law Lords issued the following statement titled "Practice Statement (Judicial Precedent)". It is to be found in ***[1966] 1 WLR 1234***. Here it is:

"Their Lordships regard the use of precedent as an indispensable foundation upon which to decide what is the law and its application to individual cases. It provides at least some degree of certainty upon which individuals can rely in the conduct of their affairs, as well as a basis for orderly development of legal rules.

Their Lordships nevertheless recognise that too rigid adherence to precedent may lead to injustice in a particular case and also unduly restrict the proper development of the law. They propose, therefore, to modify their present practice and, while treating former decisions of this House as normally binding, to depart from a previous decision when it appears right to do so.

In this connection they will bear in mind the danger of disturbing retrospectively the basis on which contracts, settlements of property and fiscal arrangements have

> been entered into and also the especial need for certainty as to the criminal law.
>
> This announcement is not intended to affect the use of precedent elsewhere than in this House".

Thus far the position in England has been looked at. The position in the United States summed up as follows by Robert S. Summers in his essay "Precedent in the United States (New York State)" which is to be found in *"Interpreting Precedents - A Comparative Study"* edited by McCormick & Summers:

> "Common law precedent in such areas as contract, torts and property is, as a matter of court practice, considered to be formally binding, or to have force, or to provide support and so on, and thus generally qualifies as a genuinely independent 'source of law' in the American states. As such, it does not require an ultimate basis or foundation in statute law or custom or any other source. Prior statutory interpretations and previous constructions of constitutional provisions in litigated cases are likewise considered to be precedent, both for the courts lower in the hierarchy and for the court that decided the precedent.
>
> At the appellate level, precedents concerning the interpretation of the state constitution seem to be somewhat less binding on appellate judges than are other precedents. See In *re Estate of Eckart,* 39 N.Y.2d 493, 499 (1976) ('In cases involving

> error in the construction of the Constitution or a statute, for sound reasons of policy and practicality, courts are generally more reluctant to change the statutory rule than the constitutional one'). By comparison, as a general matter, precedents dealing with areas of private law such as property, contracts, wills, trusts and commercial transactions are generally followed with greater regularity in appellate courts. See, for example, *Heyert v. Orange & Rockland Utilities, Inc.,* 17 N.Y.2d 352, 360-61 (1966); In *re Estate of Eckart,* 39 N.Y.2d 493; *Madfes v. Beverly Development Corp.,* 251 N.Y. 12 (1929). Moreover, precedents based upon the proper interpretation of a statute appear to have greater force in appellate courts than common law precedents dealing with areas of private law".

In India the position was stated as follows by the court in *Philip Jeya Singh v The Joint Registrar of Cooperative Societies (1992) 2 Mad. LJ 309*:

> "The following principles can be culled out from the myriad case laws. (a) A Single Judge is bound by the decision of a Division Bench and if he does not agree with it, he shall refer the matter to a larger Bench. (b) *A fortiori,* he is bound by the judgment of a Full Bench and if he does not agree with its ratio, he shall place the papers before the Chief Justice to consider whether a larger Bench should be constituted for

considering the question. (c) A Division Bench is bound by the decision of another Division Bench and if it wants to differ, it shall refer the matter to the Full Bench. (d) *A fortiori* a Division Bench is bound by the decision of a Full Bench and if it wants to differ, it shall place the papers before the Chief Justice to consider whether a larger Bench should be constituted for reconsidering the question. (e) The decision of a Full Bench is binding on the court including a subsequent Full Bench until it is overruled by a higher Court or a larger Bench. (f) A decision of a Full Bench can be reconsidered only by a larger Bench specially constituted by the Chief Justice for deciding the question. (g) Even the *obiter dictum* of a Full Bench is entitled to great weight. (h) The binding effect of a prior decision does not depend upon whether a particular argument was considered therein or not, provided that the point with reference to which an argument was subsequently advanced was actually decided. (i) the decision of the Supreme Court is binding on the High Court and the latter cannot ignore it on the ground that some relevant provisions of law were not brought to the notice of the Supreme Court or some aspects of the matter in question were not considered by the Supreme Court".

In Malaysia, the Federal Court is the apex court and its decisions are binding on all courts below it.

The next lower tier is the Court of Appeal whose decisions are binding on itself and on the courts below it. The High Court is immediately below the Court of Appeal and exercises both original and appellate jurisdiction. The decision of one High Court does not bind another High Court. But decisions of the High Court, where there is no decision of the Court of Appeal or the Federal Court are binding on the Subordinate Courts which are made up of the sessions court and the magistrate's court which are at the lowest tier of the judicature.

To sum up, the effect of the common law doctrine of binding precedent is that it is necessary for each lower tier to accept loyally the decision of the higher tiers.

3. THE ROLE OF PRECEDENT

3.1. Judge-made Law

The doctrine of binding precedent is based on the premise that judges make law. In England almost the whole of the law of contract and tort consists of judge-made law or "the common law". In India and Malaysia the law of contract is governed by an Act of Parliament. In India it is called the Indian Contract 1872. In Malaysia it is known as the Contract Act 1950. Both Acts have identical provisions though differently numbered and were introduced by the British. But the law of tort in both jurisdictions is made up largely if not entirely of a body of judge-made laws. It is of course based on the English common law. Let me give an example of judicial law making.

In *Union of India v Untied India Insurance AIR 1998 SC 640*, the facts were these. On 9 May 1979, at about 3 pm an accident happened at an unmanned and un-gated railway level crossing at Akaparamba (near Kalady) in Kerala. A bus carrying passengers was struck by the Jayanthi Janatha Express. Several passengers in the bus as well as its driver were killed. Two important questions arose. First, whether there is a duty on the driver of a vehicle approaching an unmanned and un-gated railway crossing to stop, see, listen *and get down* before proceeding to drive across the track at the level crossing. Second, whether the Railways owe a duty to take reasonable care both at common law and under statute (the Railways Act, 1890). The Supreme Court answered the first question in this way. It said that there was a duty to stop, see, listen but no duty to *get down* from the vehicle and check before proceeding. In respect of the first question, Jagannadha Rao J, a very learned judge said this:

> "In our opinion, in the absence of a board statutorily requiring the vehicle to 'stop' and the conductor to 'get down', there was only an ordinary common law duty as applicable to prudent persons. This was a duty to 'stop' 'see' and 'hear' and find out if any train was coming. It has been held by the U. S. Courts that there is no absolute duty at common law to get down from the vehicle invariably. In fact a rigid rule of getting down from the vehicle in addition to stopping, looking and hearing was laid down at one time by Justice Holmes in *Baltimore and O.R.Co. v. Goodman*, (1927) 276 UB 66 : 72 Law Ed. 167, 48 S.Ct. 24 but such a principle of special caution which

> was under adverse criticism was rejected by Cardozo, J. in *Pokora v. Wabash Rly. Co.* (1934) 292 US 98 : 78 Law Ed. 1149, 54 S.Ct. 580 stating that the requirement of getting down from the motor vehicle was good if there was a curve or an obstruction or such like situation but not when the line was straight and the train was visible. The 'get out of the car' requirement was, in the absence of special circumstances, an 'uncommon precaution, likely to be futile and sometimes even dangerous', said Cardozo, J. In our opinion, there was no duty - in the absence of a board directing the driver or conductor - to get out of the vehicle, but there was certainly a duty to stop, see and hear, at the unmanned level crossing. If that was not done, there would clearly be negligence on the part of the driver".

The Court answered the second question in the affirmative. And this what Jagannadha Rao, J said about it:

> "It has been contended for the claimants that under the common law, the Railways, as an occupier of the level crossing for the purpose of running railway trains which are inherently dangerous to those who use the public road at that point, has special responsibilities as a responsible body to see that accidents are kept at the minimum. The question then arises whether the common law duties are concurrently

enforceable along with or independently of the statutory duties under Section 13.

The law in this behalf is again well settled that the claimants can at their choice sue the railways to enforce either or both types of these duties, i.e. under common law as well as under statute. These aspects have been summarised by the Privy Council in *Commissioner for Railways v. McDermott*, (1966) 2 All ER 162 (PC). That was a case which arose from the judgment of the High Court of Australia. In that case, Lord Gardiner L.C. stated :

'Theoretically, in such a situation, there are two duties of care existing concurrently, neither displacing each other. A plaintiff could successfully sue for breaches of either or both of the duties . . . .'

It must, therefore, be accepted that the claimants can sue the Railways concurrently for breach of the common law or statutory duties or for breach of either of the duties.

The next question is as to what are the common law duties of the Railways at level crossings from time to time? In the same decision of the Privy Council in *Commissioner* for *Railways v. McDermott*, (1966) 2 All ER 162 (PC), it has been stated that the Railways duty of care at common law is based on the principle of neighbourhood laid down by Lord Atkin in *Donoghue v. Stevenson*, (1932) AC 562 inasmuch as the Railway was carrying an inherently dangerous activity of running express trains through a level crossing which was lawfully and necessarily used by local inhabitants and their guests and persons visiting them on business. Such an activity was likely to cause accidents, unless it was carried with all reasonable care. .... In principle, the liabilities are not based, however on matters of title but on the perilous nature of the operation and the *de facto* relationship which after Donoghue v. Stevenson, 1932 AC 562 would be called 'proximity' or 'neighbourly' relation between the railway operator and a substantial number of persons lawfully using the level crossing.'

The duty to care at common law is therefore based upon the dangerous or perilous nature of the operations of the railways.

In *Donoghue v. Stevenson*, (1932) AC 562 a manufacturer was held liable to the ultimate consumer at common law on the principle of duty to care. Lord Atkin said 'you must take reasonable care to avoid acts or omissions which you can reasonably foresee would be likely to injure your neighbour.' He asked : 'who, then in law is my neighbour? The answer seems to be, persons who are so closely and directly affected by my act that I ought reasonably to have them in contemplation as being so affected when I am directing my mind to the acts or omissions which are called in question.' The test of breach of common law duty is again the test of a reasonable or prudent person in the particular fact situation.

Of course the amount of care, skill, diligence or the like, varying according to the circumstances of the particular case. The standard of foresight is again that of a reasonable person. Such a person is also expected to take into account common negligence in human behaviour. Of course, he need not anticipate folly in all its forms (*London Passenger Transport Board v. Upson*, (1949) AC 155 (HL)). That if there is omission to exercise such a common law duty of care, an action at common law can be filed for non-feasance is also clear from a judgment of this Court in *Jay Laxmi Salt Works (P) Ltd. v. State of Gujarat*, (1994) 4 SCC 1. In our view, therefore, because the Railways are involved in what is recognised as dangerous or perilous operations, they are at common law, to take reasonable and necessary care, on the 'neighbourhood' principle - even if the provisions in Section 13(c) and (d) of the Railways Act, 1890 are not attracted for want of requisition by the Central Government".

In ruling that there is no duty on a motorist to get down from his vehicle to check if a train was approaching, the Supreme Court was making law.

This is because the future conduct of drivers of motor vehicles at an unmanned and un-gated rail crossing will be governed by this decision. Again, when stating that the Railways owed a duty of care to other users of the rail track because of the dangerous activity being carried on by the Railways, the Court was laying down the law in India by relying on English and Australian decisions. In this way, the Supreme Court was establishing the uniformity of the common law of the Commonwealth. This assists investors who move from one Commonwealth country to another because they are assured that in the main the common law of the country they are investing in is the same as the common law of their country of origin.

Another instance of judge-made law arises when a judge interprets an Act of Parliament. Because it is the court that determines what Parliament meant to communicate to the world at large through a particular provision. That the interpretation of statutes is the source of judge-made law has been recognised by the judges themselves. In *Velayudhan Ramakrishnan v Rajeev AIR 1989 Ker 12*, K. Sukumaran, J. said:

> "There, and then comes the role of the Court: the role as described by Lord Scarman in *Furniss v. Dawson*, 1984 STC 153:
>
> 'Whatever a statute may provide, it has to be interpreted and applied by the Courts: and ultimately it will prove to be in this area of judge-made law that our elusive journey's end will be found'.

At one time, it was thought to be sacrilegious to suggest that judges made law. It was said that judges only declare what the law has always been. The great English jurist Blackstone is credited to be the author of this theory. However, Lord Reid in an article titled "The Judge as Law Maker" published by the Journal of the Society of Professional Teaching Lawyers (JSPTL) said this:

> "There was a time when it was thought almost indecent to suggest that judges make law – they only declare it. But we do not believe in fairy tales any more".

To wind up this point, what needs to be mentioned is that there is judicial acceptance that the common law constitutes an authoritative source of law. In *Bengal Immunity Co Ltd v State of Bihar AIR 1955 SC 661*, Venkatarama Ayyar, J. said that it was:

> "necessary to bear in mind that next to legislative enactments, it is decisions of Courts that form the most important source of law. It is on the faith of decisions that rights are acquired and obligations incurred, and States and subjects alike shape their course of action".

The observation of Venkatarama Ayyar, J. that the common law comes only after Acts of Parliament is not a universal truth. It holds good in a country like England that has an unwritten constitution where Parliament is the supreme law making body with the courts having no power to strike down statutes. This is encapsulated in the following statement by Lord Macnaghten in *Vacher & Sons Ltd v London Society of Compositors [1913] AC 107, 118*:

> "Some people may think the policy of the Act unwise and even dangerous to the community. Some may think it at variance with principles which have long been held sacred. But a judicial tribunal has nothing to do with the policy of any Act which it may be called upon to interpret. That may be a matter for private judgment. The duty of the court, and its only duty, is to expound the language of the Act in accordance with the settled rules of construction. It is, I apprehend, as unwise as it is unprofitable to cavil at the policy of an Act of Parliament, or to pass a covert censure on the Legislature".

But this is not the case in a country such as India or Malaysia which has a written constitution which is the supreme law. Indeed, Article 4(1) of the Federal Constitution of Malaysia expressly provides as follows:

> "This Constitution is the supreme law of the Federation and any law passed after Merdeka Day which is inconsistent with this Constitution shall, to the extent of the inconsistency, be void".

The Indian and Malaysian courts therefore have the power (absent in an English court) to strike down Acts of Parliament as offending the Constitution. In India this power has been exercised on numerous occasions. Hence, it may be more accurate to say that judge-made law is next to a statute save where the validity of that statute is itself under challenge.

3.2. Advantage of Precedent

The doctrine of precedent when properly adhered to is very useful because it ensures certainty. This is very important to practising members of the legal profession who have to advise their clients on whether to institute an action or to defend it. But for the doctrine of precedent there would be chaos because members of the legal profession will not know what the law is and they will be unable to advise their clients. Members of the public need to know what the law is so that they may arrange their affairs in accordance with law and not in violation of it.

Many judges have spoken about this. In *Duport Steels Ltd v Sirs [1980] 1 WLR 142* Lord Scarman put it this way:

> "In our society the judges have in some aspects of their work a discretionary power to do justice so wide that they may be regarded as lawmakers. The common law and equity, both of them in essence systems of private law, are fields where, subject to the increasing intrusion of statute law, society has been content to allow the judges to formulate and develop the law. The judges, even in this, their very own field of creative endeavour, have accepted, in the interests of certainty, the self-denying ordinance of *stare decisis*, the doctrine of binding precedent; and no doubt this judicially imposed limitation on judicial lawmaking has helped to maintain confidence in the certainty and even-handedness of the law".

So too, Venkatarama Ayyar, J. said in the *Bengal Immunity* case:

> "But one principle stands out prominently above the rest, and that is that in general, there should be finality in the decisions of the highest Courts in the land, and that is for the benefit and protection of the public....... It must greatly impair the value of the decisions of this Court, if the notion came to be entertained that there was nothing certain or final about them, which must be the consequence if the points decided therein came to be reconsidered on the merits every time they were raised".

3.3. The Downside

One of the serious disadvantages of precedent is that it locks one down to a decision which produces injustice. There is nothing you can do about it. It can be very frustrating.

Let me give an illustration each from two jurisdictions. First, England. In 1893, the rule was formulated that absent a contract, the maker of careless statements is not liable to a person who relies on it and suffers purely financial loss. It was in the case of *Le Lievre v Gould [1893] 1 QB 491* which interpreted the earlier decision of the House of Lords in *Derry v. Peek (1889) 14 AC 337* as supporting the proposition. The facts of *Lievre v Gould* were as follows :

The plaintiff's were mortgagees. They lent money progressively to a builder relying on certificates issued from time to time by a surveyor setting out the stage at which buildings had been constructed. In his certificates the surveyor negligently stated the progress of the buildings. The builder defaulted and the mortgagee sued the surveyor for negligence. The English Court of Appeal held that as there was no contract between the surveyor and the mortgagee the former was not liable to the latter for the negligent misstatements he had made. Lord Esher said that although :

> "the defendant, though he had acted negligently, had not wilfully made any false statement, or been guilty of any fraud. All that he had done was to give untrue certificates negligently. Such negligence, in the absence of contract with the plaintiffs, can give no right of action at law or in equity".

That is a patently unjust result. But it held the field for 71 years. An unsuccessful attempt was made by Lord Denning (he was then Denning LJ) in *Candler v Crane, Christmas & Co [1951] 2 KB 164*. But the majority of the Court of Appeal would have none of that. They said that they were bound to follow *Lievre v Gould* as it was a binding precedent. *Candler* was a case in which the plaintiff had invested £2000 in a company relying on a set of accounts that had been negligently prepared by accountants who knew that the purpose of the accounts was to induce the plaintiff to make the investment. Counsel for the accountants argued that never before had liability been found in such a case and that it would be novel to do so. In answering the argument Denning LJ (who was in the minority) said:

> "This argument about the novelty of the action does not appeal to me. It has been put forward in all the great cases which have been milestones of progress in our law, and it has nearly always been rejected.
>
> ....
>
> On the one side there were the timorous souls who were fearful of allowing a new cause of action. On the other side there were the bold spirits who were ready to allow it if justice so required. It was fortunate for the common law that the progressive view prevailed".

Finally, in 1964, in *Hedley Byrne & Co Ltd v Heller & Partner Ltd [1964] AC 465*, the House of Lords jettisoned *Lievre v Gould* and recognised that the dissenting judgment of Denning LJ was right. As you can see, the rule of binding precedent resulted in an unjust rule remaining in the law books for almost three-quarters of a century. So much for England.

Indian citizenry too have suffered as a result of a bad precedent. The subject matter was far more serious than a mere action for negligence. It had to do with the liberty of the subject.

In *AK Gopalan v The State of Madras AIR 1950 SC 27*, it was argued that the expression "law" in Article 21 of the Indian Constitution was not confined to written law but included the rules of natural justice. That argument was rejected by a majority of the Supreme Court. Kania, C.J., whose views were echoed by those who joined him to form the majority said:

> "However, the correct question is what is

the right given by Art. 21? The only right is that no person shall be deprived of his life or liberty except according to procedure established by law. One may like that right to cover a larger area, but to give such a right is not the function of the Court; it is the function of the Constitution. To read the word 'law' as meaning rules of natural justice will land one in difficulties because the rules of natural justice, as regards procedure, are nowhere defined and in my opinion the Constitution cannot be read as laying down a vague standard. This is particularly so when in omitting to adopt "due process of law" it was considered that the expression "procedure established by law" made the standard specific. It cannot be specific except by reading the expression as meaning procedure prescribed by the legislature. The word 'law' as used in this part has different shades of meaning but in no other Article it appears to bear the indefinite meaning of natural justice. If so, there appears no reason why in this Article it should receive this peculiar meaning. Article 31 which is also in Part III and relates to the fundamental rights in respect of property runs as follows : 'No person shall be deprived of his property save by authority of law.'

It is obvious that in that clause 'law' must mean enacted law. The object of dealing with property under a different Article appears more to provide the exceptions

> found in Art. 31 (2) to (6), rather than to give the word law a different meaning than the one given in Art. 21. The word 'established' according to the Oxford Dictionary means 'to fix, settle, institute or ordain by enactment or agreement. The word 'established' itself suggests an agency which fixes the limits. According to the dictionary this agency can be either the legislature or an agreement between the parties. There is therefore no justification to give the meaning of 'jus' to 'law' in Art. 21".

This narrow and pedantic view held the field for more than a quarter of a century; 28 years later, the serious error in the reasoning in *Gopalan* was set right. It was in the case of *Maneka Gandhi v Union of India and Anor AIR 1978 SC 597* where it was held that the phrase "procedure established" referred to a fair and just procedure which accorded with the rules of natural justice so that a law that did not provide such a procedure was *ultra vires* Article 21 and void.

The Privy Council in *Ong Ah Chuan v Public Prosecutor [1981] AC 648* shows beyond the shadow of a doubt that *Gopalan* was wrongly decided. That was a case from Singapore whose Constitution has two Articles that were considered by their Lordships of the Privy Council. The two Articles are as follows:

> Article 9 (1): "No person shall be deprived of his life or personal liberty save in accordance with law.
>
> Article 12 (1): "All persons are equal before

the law and entitled to the equal protection of the law".

Notice the striking similarity between these two Articles and Articles 14 and 21 of the Indian Constitution. They all use the expression "law". Lord Diplock explained the meaning of "law" as follows:

> "[T]heir Lordships are unable to accept the narrow view cf the effect of articles 9 (1) and 12 (1) of the Constitution for which counsel for the Public Prosecutor contended. This was that since "written law" is defined in article 2 (1) to mean "this Constitution and all Acts and Ordinances and subsidiary legislation for the time being in force in Singapore" and "law" is defined as including "written law," the requirements of the Constitution are satisfied if the deprivation of life or liberty complained of has been carried out in accordance with provisions contained in any Act passed by the Parliament of Singapore, however arbitrary or contrary to fundamental rules of natural justice the provisions of such Act may be. To the full breadth of this contention one limitation only was conceded: the arbitrariness, the disregard of fundamental rules of natural justice for which the Act provides, must be of general application to all citizens of Singapore so as to avoid falling foul of the anti-discriminatory provisions of article 12 (1).
>
> Even on the most literalist approach to the construction of the Constitution this

argument in their Lordships' view involves the logical fallacy of *petitio principii*. The definition of "written law" includes provisions of Acts passed by the Parliament of Singapore only to the extent that they are "for the time being in force in Singapore"; and article 4 provides that "any law enacted by the legislature after the commencement of this Constitution which is inconsistent with this Constitution shall, to the extent of the inconsistency, be void." So the use of the expression "law" in articles 9 (1) and 12 (1) does not, in the event of challenge, relieve the court of its duty to determine whether the provisions of an Act of Parliament passed after September 16, 1963, and relied upon to justify depriving a person of his life or liberty are inconsistent with the Constitution and consequently void.

In a Constitution founded on the Westminster model and particularly in that part of it that purports to assure to all individual citizens the continued enjoyment of fundamental liberties or rights, references to "law" in such contexts as "in accordance with law," "equality before the law," "protection of the law" and the like, in their Lordships' view, refer to a system of law which incorporates those fundamental rules of natural justice that had formed part and parcel of the common law of England that was in operation in Singapore at the commencement of the

> *Constitution.* It would have been taken for granted by the makers of the Constitution that the "law" to which citizens could have recourse for the protection of fundamental liberties assured to them by the Constitution would be a system of law that did not flout those fundamental rules. If it were otherwise it would be misuse of language to speak of law as something which affords "protection" for the individual in the enjoyment of his fundamental liberties, and the purported entrenchment (by article 5) of articles 9 (1) and 12 (1) would be little better than a mockery". [Emphasis added.]

Two points need to be added for completeness. First the Union of India has a Westminster modelled constitution. Second, the fundamental rules of natural justice were very much in operation in India when the Constitution came into force.

3.4. The Value of Precedent

Once a case decides a point of law it becomes necessary in the interest of certainty that it be followed. That is the whole point about precedent. It does not always have to be a decision of the highest or apex court. Sometimes, a High Court (as a court of first instance) may lay down a principle that is followed in several later cases so that it becomes bedrock from which no departure is possible. The English law of trusts has many examples of such cases. But let me give an Indian case in the field of criminal law by way of illustration. It is the decision of the High Court at Patna in a case reported in 1930.

The name of the case is *Harakrishna Mahatab v Emperor* and it is to be found in *AIR 1930 Patna 209*. It is considered to be one of the most important cases decided on the offence of criminal breach of trust as defined by section 405 of the Indian Penal Code. It established two propositions. First, that it is neither necessary nor feasible for the prosecution to prove the precise manner in which an accused committed criminal breach of trust of property entrusted to him. Second, that mere retention of property belonging to another is not criminal breach of trust unless it is accompanied by other circumstances that supported the inference of dishonest misappropriation. The judgment in that case was delivered by Fazl Ali, J. and this is what he said:

> "It is not necessary or possible in every case of criminal breach of trust to prove in what precise manner the money was spent or appropriated by the accused, because under the law even temporary retention is an offence provided that it is dishonest; but the essential thing to be proved in case of criminal breach of trust is whether the accused was actuated by dishonest intentions or not. As the question of intention is not a matter of direct proof, the courts have from time to time laid down certain broad tests which would generally afford useful guidance in deciding whether in a particular case the accused had *mens rea* for the crime. So in cases of criminal breach of trust the failure to account for the money proved to have been received by the accused or giving a false account as

> to its use is generally considered to be a strong circumstance against the accused. We should however not lose sight of the principle and make a universal formula of what is after all only an indication of or a piece of evidence pointing to dishonest intention".

Now, although this is a case decided by a High Court, it has been repeatedly applied by the highest courts both in India and Malaysia. So the decision in *Harakrishna Mahatab* is valuable as a precedent. On the other hand, a case may have little or no value even though it was decided by the apex court of a country. Let me give an illustration in the law of contract.

It is a general rule in the law of contract that if, without justification, you break your promise in its entirety, that is to say in a fundamental a way, then your obligation to perform your promise is substituted in law by an obligation on your part to compensate the other party. All the terms in the contract cease to exist except for the purpose of determining the amount of compensation. Lord Reid put it very well in *Moschi v Lep Air Services Ltd [1973] AC 331*:

> "...I cannot agree that after accepted repudiation the contractual obligations still exist as obligations. For the breach of any contract the normal remedy is damages in money. The contract may have been to deliver say 100 tons of wheat. If the party fails to deliver somehow that obligation disappears and by operation of law is replaced by an obligation to pay money.

> So it appears to me that when a contract is brought to an end by repudiation accepted by the other party all the obligations in the contract come to an end and they are replaced by operation of law by an obligation to pay money damages. The damages are assessed by reference to the old obligations but the old obligations no longer exist as obligations. Were it otherwise there would be in existence simultaneously two obligations, one to perform the contract and the other to pay damages. But that could not be right. The only legal nexus remaining is the obligation to pay the damages..."

In *Jureidini v National British and Irish Millers Insurance Co Ltd [1915] AC 499*, the general rule that a fundamental breach puts an end to all obligations seems to have been taken too far. The speeches of the learned Law Lords in that case seem to suggest that even an arbitration clause will not survive a fundamental breach. Look at what the Lord Chancellor Viscount Haldane had to say about the point:

> "Now, my Lords, speaking for myself, when there is a repudiation which goes to the substance of the whole contract I do not see how the person setting up that repudiation can be entitled to insist on a subordinate term of the contract still being enforced".

What then is the point of putting in an arbitration clause in a contract if you cannot enforce it against the co-contractor when a dispute arises as to whether he has fundamentally breached the contract? It would render academic the whole law of arbitration. However, in *Heyman v Darwins Ltd [1942] AC 356* the House of Lords sought to distance itself from its decision in *Jureidini*. That was at a time when the House of Lords was bound by its own decisions and could not depart from them. So it adopted the approach of merely re-stating the law in such a way that demonstrated that *Jureidini* had been wrongly decided without actually overruling it. Lord Macmillan put it this way:

> "I venture to think that not enough attention has been directed to the true nature and function of an arbitration clause in a contract. It is quite distinct from the other clauses. The other clauses set out the obligations which the parties undertake towards each other *hinc inde*, but the arbitration clause does not impose on one of the parties an obligation in favour of the other. It embodies the agreement of both parties that, if any dispute arises with regard to the obligations which the one party has undertaken to the other, such dispute shall be settled by a tribunal of their own constitution. And there is this very material difference, that whereas in an ordinary contract the obligations of the parties to each other cannot in general be specifically enforced and breach of them results only in damages, the arbitration clause can be specifically enforced by the machinery of the Arbitration Acts. The

> appropriate remedy for breach of the agreement to arbitrate is not damages, but its enforcement. Moreover, there is the further significant difference that the courts in England have a discretionary power of dispensation as regards arbitration clauses which they do not possess as regards the other clauses of contracts.
>
> I am, accordingly, of opinion that what is commonly called repudiation or total breach of a contract, whether acquiesced in by the other party or not, does not abrogate the contract, though it may relieve the injured party of the duty of further fulfilling the obligations which he has by the contract undertaken to the repudiating party. The contract is not put out of existence, though all further performance of the obligations undertaken by each party in favour of the other may cease. It survives for the purpose of measuring the claims arising out of the breach, and the arbitration clause survives for determining the mode of their settlement. The purposes of the contract have failed, but the arbitration clause is not one of the purposes of the contract".

So, after *Heyman v Darwins* the decision in *Jureidini* has no value as a binding precedent. Later cases have simply not followed it.

3.5. Cross-Pollination of Precedents

In the case of *Union of India v Untied India Insurance* you saw how the decisions of the New York

Court of Appeals, of the Privy Council and of the House of Lords have had an effect on Indian jurisprudence. So, for a lawyer to effectively put across a persuasive argument and for a judge to arrive at a concluded view it is important for them to have access to the judgments of courts of other jurisdictions. As judges it is by learning from others that we can fashion the best for our jurisdiction. A lawyer or judge who lives like a frog in a well will not bring progressive change to the common law of his country. The cross-pollination of precedents can have a beneficial effect. Of course, they can also have a negative effect. Here is an illustration.

In the case of *Government of Malaysia & Ors v Loh Wai Kong [1979] 2 MLJ 33*, the Federal Court of Malaysia handed down a retrogressive decision based entirely on the majority judgments in *A.K. Gopalan*. Let me quote from the judgment of Lord President Suffian:

> "Article 5(1) speaks of personal liberty, not of *liberty simpliciter*. Does personal liberty include the three liberties? It is well-settled that the meaning of words used in any portion of a statute — and the same principle applies to a constitution — depends on the context in which they are placed, that words used in an Act take their colour from the context in which they appear and that they may be given a wider or more restricted meaning than they ordinarily bear if the context requires it. In the light of this principle, in construing "personal liberty" in article 5(1) one must

look at the other clauses of the article, and doing so we are convinced that the article only guarantees a person, citizen or otherwise, except an enemy alien, freedom from being "unlawfully detained"; the right, if he is arrested, to be informed as soon as may be on the grounds of his arrest and to consult and be defended by his own lawyer; the right to be released without undue delay and in any case within 24 hours to be produced before a magistrate; and the right not to be further detained in custody without the magistrate's authority. It will be observed that these are all rights relating to the person or body of the individual, and do not, in our judgment, include the right to travel overseas and to a passport. Indeed freedom of movement is dealt with specifically in article 9 which, however, only guarantees the citizen (but not the non-citizen) the right to enter Malaysia, and, subject to the special immigration laws applying in Sabah and Sarawak and to other exceptions set out therein, to move freely within the Federation and to reside anywhere therein. With respect, we agree with what Mukherjee, J. said at page 96 in *Gopalan* AIR 1950 SC 27:

'In ordinary language, 'personal liberty' means liberty relating to or concerning the person or body of the individual, and 'personal liberty' in this sense is the antithesis of physical restraint or coercion. According to Dicey, who is an acknowledged

> authority on the subject, 'personal liberty' means a personal right not to be subjected to imprisonment, arrest or other physical coercion in any manner that does not admit of legal justification: vide *Dicey on Constitutional Law*, Edition 9. pages 207, 208. It is, in my opinion, this negative right of not being subjected to any form of physical restraint or coercion that constitutes the essence of personal liberty.'

While the constitution by article 9 expressly gives the citizen, subject to the limitations set out therein, freedom to move freely within the country and to reside anywhere in it, it is silent as to the citizen's right to leave the country, travel overseas and have a passport for that purpose, and accordingly, in our judgment, the citizen has no constitutional right to leave the country and travel overseas".

As you can see, the narrow and restrictive interpretation of the phrase "personal liberty" by Mukherjee, J. in *Gopalan* found favour with a 5 man Bench of the Federal Court.

4. CONCLUSION

Adherence to precedent is, generally speaking, a good thing. But one should not take it to the point of no return from injustice. There are two quotations that sum-up the case against strict adherence to the stranglehold of *stare decisis*. The first is from the dissenting judgment of Scott J in *Van Kleeck v Ramer (1916) 156 Pac. 1108*:

> "I may be permitted to suggest, for the consideration of courts and judges who feel

impelled to sacrifice their sense of reason and justice upon the altar of the Golden Calf of precedent, the quaint philosophy of Sam Walter Foss, in the following lines:

'One day through the primeval wood
A calf walked home, as good calves should;
But left a trail all bent askew,
A crooked trail, as all calves do.

Since then, three hundred years have fled,
And, I infer, the calf is dead.
But still he left behind this trail,
And thereby hangs my moral tale.

The trail was taken up next day

By a lone dog that passed that way;

And then a wise bell-wether sheep
Pursued the trail o'er vale and steep,

And drew the flock behind him, too,
As good bell-wethers always do.

So from that day, o'er hill and glade,
Through those old woods a path was made,

And many men wound in and out,
And bent and turned and dodged about,
And uttered words of righteous wrath,
Because 'twas such a crooked path;

But still they followed—do not laugh—

The first migrations of that calf,
And through this winding woodway stalked
Because he wabbled when he walked.

This forest path became a lane,
That bent and turned and turned again;
This crooked lane became a road,
Where many a poor horse, with his load,

Toiled on, beneath the burning sun,
And traveled some three miles in one.
And thus a century and a half
They trod the footsteps of that calf.

The years passed on with swiftness fleet,
The road became a village street,
And this, before men were aware,
A city's crowded thoroughfare.

And soon the central street was this
Of a renowned metropolis,
And men two centuries and a half
Trod the footsteps of that calf.

Each day a hundred thousand rout
Followed the zigzag calf about;
And o'er his crooked journey went
The traffic of a continent.

A hundred thousand men were led
By one calf near three centuries dead.
They followed still his crooked way,
And lost one hundred years a day;

For thus such reverence is lent
To well-established precedent.
A moral lesson this might teach,
Were I ordained and called to preach.
For men are prone to go it blind
Along the calf-paths of the mind,
And toil away from sun to sun
To do what other men have done.
They follow in the beaten track,
And out and in, and forth and back,
And still their devious course pursue
To keep the path that others do.

But how the wise old wood-gods laugh,
Who saw the first primeval calf!

Ah! many things this tale might teach;
But I am not ordained to preach'.

The second is Lord Denning's famous dissent in *Ostime v Australian Mutual Provident Society [1960] AC 459*:

> "The doctrine of precedent does not compel your Lordships to follow the wrong path until you fall over the edge of the cliff. As soon as you find that you are going in the wrong direction, you must at least be permitted to strike off in the right direction, even if you are not allowed to retrace your steps. And that is what I would ask your Lordships to do".

I have taken quite some time to discuss the value and role of the doctrine of precedent in the common law system because, as I have already pointed out, it is that doctrine which calls for information support for the legal profession. This very paper makes the point. Look at the authorities I have referred to. Each of them - whether textbook or law report - was of vital importance to demonstrate the absolute necessity for information support. Without that support this paper would have been impossible.

Lecture 2

INFORMATION SUPPORT FOR THE LEGAL PROFESSION : AN HISTORICAL PERSPECTIVE

I have in the first lecture attempted to demonstrate the role and value of precedent. In this lecture I shall try and trace the history of information support for the legal profession.

The earliest record in the Commonwealth of lawyers collecting cases for use in court appears to be in the 1220s. Courts in those days kept records called the Rolls of the Court. They were in the form of manuscripts on parchment - the first attempt at keeping a permanent record of litigation. Usually they contained the brief facts of the case, the kind of writ that was sought (e.g., the writ of trespass) and the decision of the court. However, the exchange between lawyers (then known as serjeants-at-law) and the Bench were not written down though this often reflected the reasons why the court was deciding a case in a particular way. Also, in those days, there were no written pleadings. All litigants pleaded their cases orally. So, there was no record of what precisely the claim and the defence to that claim was. Also, during that period in English history, a litigant could lose his case if his lawyer chose the wrong form of action, e.g., if he chose the writ of trespass instead of the writ of ejectment. Much emphasis was placed on form rather than substance. But, though a lawyer may get the form right, yet, it would be important for him to have information about how a similar case had been dealt with by the King's justices. And so was born the doctrine of precedent.

Baker sums up the position as follows in his "*Introduction to English Legal History*" (4th edn.):

> "A lawyer practising in the king's courts needed to know much more than the bare routine formulae. He needed to know how the courts worked. Although this could only be learned by experience, as early as the 1220s lawyers were extracting interesting cases from the plea rolls as illustrations of the law, and many such cases were used by the author of the treatise called *Bracton*. The rolls continued to be the most authoritative source of precedents into later times, and it was common for counsel to 'vouch the record' when citing a previous case. But the record was highly formulaic, using stereotyped Latin phrases in place of detailed assertions, omitting the evidence, the arguments of counsel, and the reasons for judgments. The debates between the serjeants and judges, the tentative pleading and judicial rulings which obliquely revealed the assumptions of the

> common law, took place off the record, and only the formalised results went down on parchment. For those learning the law, these forensic exchanges were naturally of greater importance than the bare record. Long attendance in Westminster Hall was therefore an indispensable part of a common lawyer's education. The natural store for such learning was the human mind. Royal judges of the twelfth and thirteenth centuries must have relied heavily on memory and experience, prompted by the rolls. But memory is frail and unsafe, and if continuity was to be preserved from one generation to another, and if legal discussions in the Bench were to reach a wider audience than those who happened to hear them in court, then some additional kind of record was required".

The first ever law reports are called "Year Books". It appears that they first came on the scene from about 1250. But they are not law reports in the sense we know them today. They were a mixed bag of statements by judges made in different cases that came before the King's Courts. However, from about 1291 there was a continuous reporting of arguments that took place in the Court of Common Pleas. We do not know who the authors of these reports were. These reports however carried the names of the speakers during the court proceedings. Sometimes the author's comments were added. The writs that issued were all in Latin. Let me give you an example taken from a case on contract. It is the case of *Waldon v. Marshall* which was decided in 1370. The writ issued by one William Waldon against John Marshall alleged as follows:

> "quod praedictus Johannes manucepit equum praediciti Willelmi de infirrnitate, et postea praedictus Johannes ita negligenter curam suam fecit quod equus suus interiit".

When translated the sense of the passage is more or less as follows:

> "that the aforesaid John took in hand and made himself responsible for the said William's horse so far as its illness is concerned, and afterwards the aforesaid John performed his cure so negligently that his horse died".

But the reports were all in Anglo-French which was the language used in courts in those days. Here is an example of a report of a case on joint tenancy:

> "Nota que si un joint estate est fait &I Baron & Feme & a Is tieree person in fee, le quel tierce person reless, tout son droit que il avoit a Is dit Baron, que adonques Is dit Baron avera Is moitie que Is tierce person avoit & Is feme do ceo nad riens & Is baron ad feesimple in ceo nient obstant que le dit tierce person no relessa, a Illy & a ces heires a touts jours Et issint ceo adjudge in Is Common Bank. Hill. 10 Viz. Reginve inter Escofte & al' in Coffi EboF. Vide Inst. in Littleton title Tenants in Common".

Even today, you can see some of the very rare Year Books on display at Lincoln's Inn Library in London. Grays Inn also had some, but they are all now lost thanks to the late lamented Herr Hitler who decided that the Inn should have some vacant space for a new library.

The law of demand and supply dictates the availability of goods in all fields of economic activity. The law is no different. It was only after the advent of the legal profession that demand for information about decided cases arose. This was during the reigns of Henry II and Edward I. But it must be said there is some doubt whether the first Year Books were meant for practitioners or their apprentices. By the middle of the 16th Century, law reporting was placed on a more official footing. Let me quote once again from Baker:

> "A long-standing tradition, beginning in about 1550, firmly attributed the year-books to official reporters, conjecturally identified by some as the prothonotaries of the Common Pleas. But this thesis is no longer accepted; there are no records of the appointment or payment of official reporters, no year-books were preserved with the records and office-books of the courts, and some of the early reports are both informal and inaccurate in matters of factual detail. The purpose of the reports cannot have been to supplement the rolls for official purposes, since they frequently omit the details such as the names of the parties - which would be needed to identify the entries in the record. The purpose must rather have been to record the intellectual aspect of litigation: to circulate and

> preserve for future learning, both by students and by their practising elders, the possible moves in the recondite games of legal chess played by the pleaders in open court. If we have to account for their beginning, the most likely explanation is that they arose from a case-method of instruction in the law school which served the apprentices of the Bench before the emergence of the inns of court. This would help to explain the anonymity of the texts; they were not individual compilations, but resulted from the communal interchange of notes generated by the teaching process. For the same reason, the contemporary value of the earliest reports lay not in their historical authenticity as precedents but in the ideas and suggestions which they contained. If one report is very different from another, we should not rush to blame it on carelessness; we may rather be seeing a teacher teasing out the points in a case by varying the facts. If that is so, it mattered little who wrote the manuscripts; any sense they made was self-evident, and any nonsense could be freely corrected or ignored by the owner".

Moving on, it appears that by the reign of Henry VIII three things happened. First, there was an increase in the reporting of cases. Second, the very nature of the reports themselves changed. One of the reasons for this is the change in the procedure of the various courts. Oral pleadings were no longer permitted. A litigant had to put his case down in writing. This led to what is called the joinder of issues of fact and law between the parties to litigation. An example of a joinder is this.

Let us suppose that the plaintiff in an action asserts in his statement of claim that he or she had made an oral agreement with the defendant. If the defendant denies the existence of such an oral agreement then the joinder is whether there was such an agreement. And that is the issue which the court has to decide. Of course, whether in given circumstances there was an oral agreement between two or more persons is a question of fact. It is really useless to a lawyer or to the court as a point of reference because the fact pattern in one case is almost always different from another

Let me give another example. A plaintiff, the owner of land in his statement of claim alleges that the defendant is trespassing on the land. The defendant in his defence says that the plaintiff does not have possession of the land and therefore cannot bring the action. Here the joinder is whether a person who is not in actual possession of land may bring a suit for trespass. This is a question of law and when decided one way or the other will be useful to the court in future cases of claims for trespass to land. This is the sort of ruling that went into the Year Books

So much for hypothetical illustrations. Let me now give you the report of an actual case. It is *Orwell v. Mortoft*. It is a very important case in the law of contract. It was decided in 1505. It is still the law. The citation of the case is *Y.B.20 Hen. VII M f 41, Keilwey*. This means that it was decided in the 20th year of the reign of Henry VII, in the Michaelmas

Term (which commences on 2 October of one year and ends on 3 January of the following year). The '*f*' is Latin for pl in English, meaning "pleading". So, *f* 41 means that the case is the 41st pleading in the report. And it was reported in the Year Book by one Keilwey who was an official reporter. In the report, Keilwey makes the following note of an opinion expressed by Fineux C. J. in 1502:

> "Where a carpenter makes a bargain to make me a house and does nothing, no action on the case lies, for it sounds in covenant. But if he makes the house improperly, the action on the case lies well".

The principle to be extracted from the above ruling is this. If the promisor in a contract fails or refuses to perform his promise altogether then the promisee can only sue him for breach of contract. The promisor cannot be sued for negligence. However, if the promisor does perform his obligation but does so carelessly, the promisee may sue him both in contract and in tort. That, as I have already said is still the law. Thus, in Midland Bank v Hett, Stubbs & Kemp (a firm) [1979] Ch 384, Oliver J held that solicitors (and this extends to other professionals such as engineers, architects and doctors) owe a concurrent duty under contract as well as in tort to perform their tasks with reasonable skill and care. So you can see how a point of law decided in the early 1500's continues to be applied from time to time right up to 500 years later. This illustrates, in the historical context, the importance of access to information in the field of law.

Let me return to the reports themselves. I was

speaking about the change in the nature of the reports themselves. Another reason for this change was the printing press which came to England in the 1470's. Within 10 years of its arrival, the first law text was printed – the famous Littleton's Tenures which was printed in 1481. It may be appropriate to mention here that Sir James Dyer, one of the well known reporters, produced a report of cases decided from 1513 to 1582. His reports are called "Dyer's Reports". They are simply cited as, for example, (1540) Dyer. Some of his reports overlap some of the later Year Books. Dyer's Reports are also called Reports from the Lost Notebooks of Sir James Dyer.

The other set of reports are what are referred to as the Nominate Reports. These cover the period 1571 to 1865. There are more than 260 of such reports. They are called "Nominate Reports" because they are named after the individuals who published the reports. They include such persons as Giffard, Plowden, Coke, Burrow, and Durnford & East. Of these, Durnford & East were the first publishers to cover the four terms of court, namely, Michaelmas, Hilary, Easter and Trinity.

The older reports are now contained in two compendious sets. One of them is called the "English Reports (Full Reprint)". There are 176 volumes of reports and 2 volumes of alphabetical table of cases. There is also a chart that comes with each set that cross refers the old reports to the English Reports by publisher and year. The English Reports contain more than 100,000 cases decided between 1220 and 1865. The publishers have taken the trouble of ensuring accuracy whenever possible. When two or more versions of the same case are available in different nominate reports the more accurate version has been selected for inclusion. The disadvantage is that the dates of the cases are not always available. The citation for English Reports is by volume followed by the abbreviation of the report and the page in the Reprint, e.g., 134 ER 213.

The other compendious set is the Revised Reports. These comprise 152 volumes of cases decided by the superior courts of England between 1786 and 1866. The Revised Reports were published between 1891 and 1920. They are accompanied by a table of cases and a subject index digest in 2 volumes. The Revised Reports are authoritative because they were edited by Sir Frederick Pollock, a jurist with close connections to India.

The printing of reports brought about some anomalies and inaccuracies as well. Baker describes it as follows:

> "Unfortunately for the historian, the magic of the printed word has tended to obscure the underlying textual tradition of the year-books. Many interesting years, including all those of Edward I and Edward II, more than ten years of Edward III and the entire reign of Richard II, were omitted altogether. In the later reigns a wide variety of texts, no longer recoverable because of manuscript losses, was confused into a deceptively uniform series. Our suspicions are aroused when we find judges speaking after they were dead, and similar chronological impossibilities; moreover, careful

> investigation shows that what are printed as different but related cases, or as successive arguments in the same case, are sometimes reports of the very same argument by different hands. The last printed year-book of all, ending with Michaelmas term 27 Henry VIII (1535), has been taken to represent some definitive line between old and new; and the cessation of the series was believed by Maitland to be an ominous event which marked the decline of the common law *at* the zenith of Henrician despotism".

There is little doubt that the Year Books provide the first signs of inclination to precedent. But there is either no, or no serious, citation of cases by lawyers or judges. The great English jurist Winfield in his seminal work *"The Chief Sources of English Legal History"* (1925) provides the following evidence of this:

"In Y. B. Mich. 34 Henry VI, at f 24*a*, Fortescue, C.J.K.B., says,

> 'If this judgment were to be given for the first time, in my opinion no judges now would like the plaintiff to recover goods belonging to the executors themselves. But because so many judgments have allowed this in a case of this sort, and because that is the law now, and usage makes the law without any other reason,' etc.

Later in the same case (at f. 24b) Prisot, C.J.C.P., said to one of the counsel,

> 'The opinion of all my companions except Moyle and Moy is that they [the executors] shall not be charged as to their own goods, and that is the opinion of several other judges in the King's Bench. Yet it seems to me against right, for I have seen the matter adjudged etc.'

Perhaps this 'etc.' was an identification of the case by name, for he gives a brief abstract of it. Fortescue thought it was ill-argued and of little weight. Two inferences may, it is suggested, be drawn from these quotations. First, we get further proof of the idea, insistent throughout the history of our law, that rules previously adopted by the judges ought to be maintained by them, and of the judges' willingness to reinforce evidence of the existence of these rules by means of previous decisions if, and when, they can get them. Second, it would be going too far to say that there is any sufficient evidence of the practice of citing cases. In fact, the lack of positive evidence in support of any such view is overwhelming. If the theory of precedent were established at this period, why is it so hard to find instances of it in the Year-Books? For other purposes we have examined closely over two hundred eases in them selected from every reign which they cover, and we cannot recollect one single citation of a case in the sense in which we understand that term. With a view to testing what was a matter of memory,

> we took the Year-Book of 39 Henry VI and went through every case in it. For this year, there are fifty-one folios, and in all there are five citations of cases which in the aggregate do not amount to a quarter of a single folio".

The non-citation of cases by counsel and the courts may be due to the informality with which a record of cases was kept. Before the advent of printing the cases were in manuscript form. These manuscripts may have been lost or destroyed. Also, it would appear that there was a fair amount of informality in the way in which records of cases were kept. The reporters were probably more concerned about getting down the point of law as perceived by them rather than keeping a record of the names of the parties or the full facts of the case or the arguments of counsel. That is why there are many cases decided during this period that carry the title "Anon" which is the short form for anonymous.

If we take into account Winfield's summary of the position, it may equally be inferred that the judges, since they were probably not hearing as many cases as today, relied more on their memory of cases decided by them or of anecdotal references brought to their attention by counsel. But what cannot be denied is the real search by lawyers and judges for information to help argue or decide cases.

There is another feature of the common law that for historical reasons underpins the requirement of information support. The common lawyer argues his case by analogy. In other words, he finds a decided case either exactly the same as or similar to the one he is arguing or deciding. It is often very difficult to find a case on all fours. This is because fact patterns vary infinitely and as has been said often enough one fact pattern is no precedent for another. So he finds a case analogous to the one he is arguing and he attempts to persuade the court that it should accept apply the prior analogy and arrive at the same conclusion. That is of course if the earlier case supports him. What if it does not? Then he also argues by analogy - seeking to distinguish the earlier case to show that it is *not* analogous to his. This is called "the incremental development" of the common law.

This may be seen very early in the history of the cases reported. Let me quote from Winfield again:

> "But what the Year-Books do show us again and again is the creation of new rules, and the extension or confirmation of old ones, by analogies from existing law and by analogies from hypothetical facts. Judges and counsel constantly make comparisons between the point of law before them and a similar point in some other department of the law. Thus, if a rule in the law of trespass is to be applied to the law of detinue, arguments will be raised on each of these topics quite independently of any particular case on trespass. Often the points so compared are in matters of procedure, which is just the branch of law that would facilitate this kind of argument by analogy. It suited exactly the mould in which medieval law was cast, where procedure is so predominant that we wonder at times

where the point of substantive law is to be found in the web of writ, declaration, counterplea, double plea, and judgment. As to imaginative variations of facts, a case several folios in length will be full of this sort of thing, without a word said about other cases that have actually occurred. Frequently this takes the form of pushing some opposite line of argument (also generally based on mere suppositions) to its logical extreme and then pointing out that this is 'against reason,' or 'will be strange.' If the judges differ from one another, they do so openly and without the least constraint, and a marked difference in the conduct of a trial then and now is their brisk open discussion among themselves and a tendency to treat counsel as their equals".

Let me now digress for a while to illustrate the point that Winfield makes. From at least the 14th century it was held that one who contracts with another to perform a service he is under a duty to act with reasonable care in performing that service. In Y.B. 43 Edw.III, M., f 38, there is noted a case decided in 1364 of a surgeon who was held liable for negligently failing to cure a horse after having undertaken to do so. Again, in YB 11 Henry IV M., f 60, there appears a case decided in 1433 of a carpenter who had been found liable for negligently building a house. Over a period of time these cases were interpreted to mean that only a person who was a party to a contract could sue if the contract was performed negligently. Third parties could not.

By the mid 1800's, this had become firmly rooted.

The leading case is *Winterbottom v. Wright* 10 M. & W. 109 [(1842) 152 E.R. 402] which ruled against product liability. In other words, the manufacturer of an article owed no duty to take reasonable care to ensure that the product was reasonably safe for use by the ultimate consumer. For those who are non-lawyers and would like to know more about the case, there is a note about it, the cases that followed it and the change in attitude of the courts in the Appendix to this paper.

A word about the original citation of the report of *Winterbottom v Wright*. M & W refers to the two publishers of the report. They were Meeson and Welsby. They only published cases decided by the Court of Exchequer and Court of Exchequer Chamber. Their reports begin in 1836 and end in 1847. All together there are about 12 volumes.

Now, if you look at the original report of *Winterbottom v. Wright* you will find the arguments of counsel reported in full. In those days, the practice was for the submissions of counsel and the interventions by the Bench to be reported. Even today, the Law Reports published by the Incorporated Council of Law Reporting for England & Wales ("the ICLR") almost always carry the arguments of counsel.

At this point it may be convenient to say a few words about the ICLR. The ICLR was established in 1865 by members of the legal profession. Its object is set out in its Memorandum and Articles of Association dated 1870 as follows:

"preparation and publication, in a

> convenient form, at a moderate price, and under gratuitous professional control, of [The Law] Reports of Judicial Decisions of the Superior and Appellate Courts in England".

The bit about the moderate price may no longer hold good thanks to inflation and the high cost of editing and printing.

Today, the ICLR publishes a number of reports. Among them are the Weekly Law Reports which began publication in 1953. It usually has 3 volumes per year. The cases published in volume 1 are customarily not published in the Law Reports published by ICLR. You know that is so because of the asterix that appears against the title of the case. But cases published in the second and third volumes are often also published in the Law Reports. Let me illustrate by reference to actual cases.

The case of *Anisminic Ltd v The Foreign Compensation Commission* is reported in the second volume of the Weekly Law Reports for the year 1969. It is to be found at page 163 of the report. This is reflected by the citation [1969] 2 WLR 163. Because it is reported in the second volume of the Weekly Law Reports, it is also reported in the Law Reports, Appeal Cases. The citation is [1969] 2 AC 147. What is the difference between the two reports? The Weekly Law Report does not carry the arguments of counsel, whereas the Appeal Cases do. The advantage is that you get to read the submissions of some of the leading luminaries in the Law and gain knowledge. We can see the cases cited by them during argument. Some of these cases may not be referred to by the judges in their judgments. However, they are invaluable for a lawyer doing research on a particular point.

Let me give another example. The case of *Alghussein Establishment v Eton College [1988] 1 WLR 587* is also a case decided by the House of Lords. As may be seen, it appears in the first volume of the Weekly Law Reports for the year 1988. It carries an asterix (which I have also added) indicating that it will not appear in the Appeal Cases.

Before moving on, let me say a word about the Appeal Cases. This report carries only cases decided by the House of Lords and the Privy Council. These are very important cases as they are decisions of the Apex court of the United Kingdom (in the case of the House of Lords) and of those Commonwealth countries that still have appeals to the Judicial Committee of the Privy Council. At one time, the Privy Council heard appeals from all British colonies, Dominions and Protectorates. These days, appeals to the Privy Council come principally from the Eastern and Western Caribbean courts and from Mauritius. Most of the other Commonwealth countries have abolished appeals to the Privy Council. Instead, they each have their own Apex Courts. The latest country to abolish appeals to the Privy Council is New Zealand which has established its own Supreme Court. So much for the historical summary of law reporting in England. I now turn to deal with the position in India.

The system of law reporting began in India after 1774 when the British East India Company established Supreme Courts in Bombay, Calcutta and Madras. Initially, there was no organised system of law reporting. The early reports were the product of private entrepreneurs. The reports were irregular and were written up by lawyers and judges. They appear to have begun in Calcutta as illustrations in local legal publications. One of the first texts on Hindu Law, a subject that appears to have fascinated British lawyers in India, is a work titled "Considerations upon Hindu Law". It was written by Sir Francis Macnaghten, a retired judge of the Calcutta Supreme Court and published in 1824. It contains only reports of some of the cases decided on points of Hindu law. In 1825, cases that had decided points of Islamic law were produced in a book titled "Dissertations on Mohammedan Law".

The next development was in 1829 when Longueville Clarke produced his Rules and Orders of the Supreme Court. These contained notes of cases decided during the course of each judicial year. Then, in 1834 Smoult's "Collection of Orders" was published. This contains notes of interesting cases decided between 1774 and 1813. These notes though brief are useful. They include cases decided on matters of civil practice from 1774 to 1798.

In the 18th and 19th centuries, a number of law reports of judgments of the Calcutta Supreme Court were published by individual reporters following the English practice of the time. These include Morton's Reports which was the earliest of the law reports covering the period 1774 to 1841.

The others are

1. Bignell's Reports for the period 1830-31;
2. Fulton's Reports which is really only one volume of judgments handed down from 1842 to 1844;

3. Montriou's Reports in two volumes published in 1846;
4. Montriou's Select Cases from the Morton's Reports;
5. Boulnois' Reports, 1853-59, in two volumes;
6. Gasper's Commercial Cases, 1851-1860 ;
7. Taylor's Reports of Cases decided from Jan. 1847 to Dec. 1848;
8. Taylor and Bell's Reports, 1847-53 (3 volumes); and
9. Gasper's Reports of Small Cause Court Cases 1850-59.

As far as Bombay was concerned, the earliest law report is Perry's Oriental Cases. It came in two volumes. The first mainly contained cases decided by the Bombay Supreme Court on the application of the English common law to India. The second volume which was in manuscript form was included in full in volume 2 of Morley's Digest of Cases. Perry (Sir Erskine Perry) was a retired Chief Justice of the Bombay Supreme Court.

Cases decided by the Supreme Court of Madras in terms of law reporting are limited to the period 1798 to 1816. They were collected and published in three volumes by Sir Thomas Strange who was Chief Justice of the Madras Supreme Court in 1816. Although Strange's Reports carried judgments in a comprehensive form, the rulings of the Supreme Court of Madras on issues of native law came to be regarded as doubtful or even inaccurate. This is because of the unavailability of proper materials for the court to arrive at a correct decision.

In the course of time the old reports of the Calcutta, Bombay and Madras Supreme Court decisions became unavailable as they went out of print. Since they contained important rulings on points of early Indian jurisprudence they were very valuable and constantly in demand. As such they were reprinted in 1911 in a set of reports in five volumes called the Indian Decisions (Old Series) which came under the editorship of one Mr. T Venkaswamy Rao. Each volume contained a reprint of the old reports. The first three volumes covered the Calcutta, Supreme Court and contained the cases reported in the old reports for the period 1774 to 1860. Each volume contained cases for a specific period. Thus the first volume had cases from 1774 to 1846; the second volume was for the period 1847 to 1859 and the third volume contained cases in the old reports for the period 1851 to 1860. In this way the original nine law reports of cases decided by the Calcutta Supreme Court were reproduced. Volume 4 contained the Bombay cases while the fifth volume had the Madras decisions. The remaining volumes which began from six onwards contained the reports of the Sadar Diwani Adalats cases. The Sadar Adalats were the apex courts created by the East India Company in respect of the Mofussil justice system. They cover the period 1791 to 1849. Apart from the Sadar Diwani Adalats in Calcutta Bombay and Madras, there was also a criminal judicature called the Sadar Nizamat Adalats. These were also established by the East India Company. The cases decided by them were reported, in respect of Calcutta, in two volumes by Sir William Macnaghten. There are three others which carry no reporters names.

Today, even the Indian Decisions (Old Series) have become difficult if not impossible to obtain as they too have gone out of print. However the Indian Decisions (Old Series) are of interest only to a legal historian as much of the early jurisprudence has been either subsumed into or overtaken by decisions coming after 1857, the two World Wars and post-Independence.

In 1862, not long after the failed Revolution of 1857, the British Government established three Chartered High Courts, one each in Madras, Bombay and Calcutta. This led to what can be considered as the forerunner of the modern era of the Indian justice system as it stands today. With the establishment of the High Courts and the passing of the Indian Law Reports Act 1875, there came the official reports called the Indian Law Reports or ILR, which is cited by volume and the respective court, for example ILR 51 Mad would refer to the 51st volume of the Indian Law Reports for the Madras High Court. It must be added that apart from the official Indian Law Reports there were also private law reports such as the Madras Jurist, the Weekly Reporter, Indian Jurist, two volumes of Hyde E. Reports, three volumes of Kinealy & Henderson Reports and fifteen volumes of Bengal Law Reports, all in respect of the High Court of Calcutta.

Further, the reports published under the Act of 1875 were extended to include other High Courts such as Allahabad in 1876, Patna in 1922, Lucknow in 1926, Nagpur in 1936, Punjab in 1948, Cuttack & Assam in

1949, Rajastan & Mysore in 1951, Andra Pradesh in 1954, Kerela in 1957 and Gujurat in 1960. Other High Courts have since been added. Although section 3 of the 1875 Act declared the ILR to be the official report, it did not prohibit the publication of private law reports or denude the authoritative nature of such private law reports. One of the earliest private law reports was the Madras Law Journal, which began in 1891 and is still in publication. The other is the Calcutta Weekly Notes, which started in 1896. The Allahabad Law Journal, which is another well known law report, commenced in 1904 and continues even today. The Bombay Law Reporter commenced publication in 1899. In 1922, what are probably the most well known law reports in India and common law countries in Southeast Asia commenced publication. It is the All India Law Reporter, cited as A.I.R. Despite it having commenced only in 1922, the A.I.R. published volumes of cases for each High Court as well as the Privy Council, and a Journal section from the year 1914. It continues till today. It is the single most comprehensive law report to come out of India. Its advantage is that each volume is tailored to carry reports from more than one High Court, although the earlier volumes, especially pre-Independence, for the Chartered High Courts, carried one volume per High Court. They are cited as, example, A.I.R. 1943 Nag 222. Prior to Partition, there was a High Court in Lahore and the A.I.R. is the only report that carries the Lahore cases even today.

At a time when there were appeals to the Privy Council two separate law reports covered cases decided by the Judicial Committee. The first was a private law report published by Mr. E.F. Moore. It was cited as M.I.A., or Moore's Indian Appeals. Moore's reports are contained in an old series and a new series. They are for the period 1836 to 1862 and are now available in volumes 12 to 15 of the English Reports. There is a second set of reports by Moore from 1836 to 1872, which are in volumes 18 to 20 of the English Law Reports. The official law report of Privy Council cases is the Law Reports Indian Appeals which is cited by volume only, e.g. L.R. 15 I.A. 21.

In addition to all the official reports there are State publications which are extremely useful for practitioners, academics and judges. They are, for example, the Andra Weekly Reporter (Andh. W.R.), the Andra Law Times (A.L.T.), the Kerela Law Times (K.L.T.) and the Punjab Reporter (P.R.). Quite apart from all these reports, there are specialist reports covering tax cases such as the Indian Tax Reporter (I.T.R.), Company Cases (Comp.Cas.), Company Law Journal (Comp. L.J.), the Calcutta Law Journal (C.L.J.), the Election Cases (E.C.) and the like.

After Republic Day and the establishment of the Supreme Court, the official law reports for cases decided by the Indian Supreme Court is the Supreme Court Reports which is cited by year and volume, e.g. [1952] 2 S.C.R. Even today, when the House of Lords or the Privy Council cites Indian Supreme Court judgments, reference is always made to the S.C.R. in preference to the A.I.R. It must be added that the A.I.R. also carries a separate volume for decisions of the Supreme Court. There is also another private law report called the Supreme Court cases, cited as S.C.C. which only deals with judgments of the Supreme Court. Discussions with serving and retired judges of the Supreme Court of India reveal that the preference in that court is to the S.C.C.

So much for a summary of law reporting in India. I now turn to Malaysia.

Law reporting began in Malaysia in the 19th Century. The very first record of an officially published judgment is in 1808. It is to be found in a set of reports known as Kyshe's Reports. Those reports contain cases decided by Her Majesty's Supreme Court of the Straits Settlements between 1808 and 1884. A word about the Straits Settlements. These were the three original British colonies in Southeast Asia. They were Singapore, Melaka and Penang. English law applied in these three colonies in every respect, including land law. So, the English concepts such as fee simple and the complicated English method of conveyancing were applied in the Straits Settlements.

The Straits Settlements Reports were reported by James Kyshe who was the Acting Registrar of the Supreme Court of the Straits Settlements in Melaka. Later, there came other reports, none of which lasted for any significant period of time.

In 1932, a man who had never set foot inside a law school published a report out of Singapore which he called *The Malayan Law Journal*. He was the late Dr. Bashir Mallal to whom every lawyer in Malaysia and Singapore owes a debt of gratitude. Today, the law report which Dr. Mallal's genius and industry produced is the leading law report in Malaysia. Its publication for sometime now has been in the capable hands of Lexis Nexis Butterworths.

Apart from the Malayan Law Journal, there are

two other reports. One of these is the *Current Law Journal* which is an entirely homegrown venture. The other is the *All Malaysia Reports*, a Thomson (Swet & Maxwell Asia) publication. Both these are fairly recent publications. A total of 18 volumes of reports are published annually by the three publishers. This is not helpful and is the product of multiple reporting of the same cases.

In the Malaysian context, when preparing a case, whether for argument or decision, it is vital for the advocate or judge, as the case may be, to be armed with information about the methodology and approach adopted by other courts of the common law heritage and tradition. This is because several of our written laws are either based upon or are a reproduction of statutes of other common law countries. Much of our common law and doctrines of equity find their origin in England. Our Evidence Act, Penal Code, Contracts Act, Specific Relief Act and Criminal Procedure Code are drawn from parallel legislation in India. Our Hire Purchase Act is drawn on the Australian model. Our securities legislation, in particular those provisions proscribing wash sales and insider trading are based upon parallel legislation in the United States and Canada. Similarly, our courts are always concerned about current developments in the law of tort in other Commonwealth jurisdictions. So, when dealing with a problem in a given area, it is essential for us to see how courts of other Commonwealth jurisdictions have interpreted similar or the same provisions. It is here that immediate access to a current body of authority is indispensable.

Long before the advent of the electronic

dissemination of information, lawyers and judges alike relied on the one-time irreplaceable *English & Empire Digest* and the *Current Law Yearbook* for assistance. Let me give you an illustration.

In *Trowell v Public Prosecutor (1946) MLJ 41*, the question arose as to the manner in which the corroboration rule was to be applied to a case tried by a judge sitting alone. Horne J found it difficult to find a case to cover such a situation as all then existing authority dealt with directions to juries. However, he was able to rely on the summary of the judgment is the Canadian case of *Rex v Ambler (1938) 2 WWR 225*, found in the English and Empire 1940 Digest Supplement, page 48.

This brings me to the next point. Often, an issue of law of considerable importance, though decided by the Privy Council, was only reported in the domestic report of the country from which the appeal came. The non-availability of the particular report would, of course close us from a valuable source of critical assistance. We in Malaysia were sometimes saved from such a situation through the citation of the particular case in the judgment of an English or an Indian court. There are examples of this. Let me give you just one.

There is the decision of the Privy Council in *American Surety Co of New York v Calgary Milling Co Ltd (1919) 48 DLR 295* which illustrates the application of the doctrine of estoppel to the meaning of a term in an agreement. It is a case that is only reported in the *Dominion Law Reports of Canada*. Lawyers in Malaysia only became aware of this rather important decision because of its *in extenso* reference in the judgment of Luxmoore J in *De Tchihatchef v Salerni Coupling Ltd [1932] 1 Ch 330*.

To conclude, as a matter of history, the printed report has proved to be the primary source of information for lawyers throughout the Commonwealth. Even in common law jurisdictions outside the Commonwealth, such as the United States and the Philippines, law reports of their respective jurisdictions have been the primary source of assistance in the decision-making process or in the classroom. American texts and cases on specific subjects such as contract, tort and trust continue to be useful to us because the primary foundation of American jurisprudence is English law. And it is the principles of English law that continue to influence all of us in the common law world.

Appendix-1

The facts of *Winterbottom v Wright* are as follows. The defendant entered into a contract with the Postmaster-General to supply mail coaches to convey mail from Hartford to Holyhead. The horses and coachmen for the journey were provided by one Atkinson. The plaintiff was one of the coachmen. The plaintiff was injured when driving one of the coaches that was defective through the defendant's negligence. He sued the defendant for damages for his injuries. He failed. The plaintiff's counsel argued that the defendant was liable because –

> "the defendant entered into a contract with a public officer to supply an article which, if imperfectly constructed, was necessarily dangerous, and which, from its nature and the use for which it was destined, was necessarily to be driven by a coachman."

In essence what was being submitted was that the manufacturer of an article owed a duty of care to the ultimate consumer. In other words, there was an invitation to the court to establish what we know today as product liability. The Court of Exchequer however dismissed the claim. It was unimpressed that the plaintiff would be remediless. One of the judges, Baron Alderson thought that the line must be drawn somewhere and that the duty of care ought to be limited to parties to a contract. This is what he said:

> "The contract in this case was made with the Postmaster-General alone; and the

> case is just the same as if he had come to the defendant and ordered a carriage, and handed it at once over to Atkinson. If we were to hold that the plaintiff could sue in such a case, there is no point at which such actions would stop. The only safe rule is to confine the right to recover to those who enter into the contract: if we go one step beyond that, there is no reason why we should not go fifty."

This view was reiterated in several subsequent cases some of which had nothing to do with product liability. I will mention one of them. It is *Alton v. Midland Ry. Co 19 C.B. N.S. 213 [(1865) 144 E.R. 768]*. The plaintiff's servant was travelling in the defendant's train when he has injured through the defendant's negligence. The plaintiff sued the defendant for damages for loss of his servant's services suffered in consequence of the defendant's negligence. The law as it then stood entitled a master to recover damages for the loss of his servant's services where the servant was intentionally injured by a defendant, through, for example, an assault. On the facts, it was the servant who had a contract with the railway company. The Court of Common Pleas, applying earlier decisions, dismissed the plaintiff's claim. It is useful to quote from the judgment of Willes J:

> "It must be admitted by the defendants that a long series of authorities has established that a master may sue for loss of services caused by a pure wrong, a trespass, to his servant, as by beating him.

> On the other hand, it is indisputable that no such action has ever been sustained in a case in which the injury to the servant was not actionable in respect of the civil wrong, but only in respect of a duty arising out of and founded upon a contract with the servant. The liability of the defendants in the case before us is of the latter kind, and falls within the principle of a series of decisions upon which there is no room for doubt. The case does not, I apprehend, fall within the principle contended for on the part of the plaintiffs, for this simple reason, because the rights founded on contract belong to the person who has stipulated for them. Here, the right to be carried safely was stipulated for by the servant it was a right acquired by him by reason of a bargain with the defendants. To hold that the plaintiffs can maintain this action would be to hold that they could acquire a right by means of a contract to which they were no parties either by themselves or by their agent."

From this strict adherence to contract as the basis of liability in negligence there began a slow change. The first step was in *George v Skivington (1869) LR 5 Exch 1* where the facts were these. The defendant was a chemist. In the course of his business he sold a bottle of hair wash which he had made to the plaintiff for use by the plaintiff's wife. The wife used it and was injured. The plaintiff and his wife sued the defendant. The contract in this case was between the husband and the defendant. The wife had no contract with the defendant although the defendant knew that the hair wash was to be used by the wife. The husband had a contract with the defendant. But it was not he who used the hair wash and suffered the injury. Applying *Winterbottom v Wright*, the plaintiffs' claim was set to fail. But it succeeded. The Court of Exchequer side stepped the issue of contract. The genius of the common law is revealed in the judgment of Kelly CB. This is what he said:

> "There was no warranty, it is said, either express or implied, towards the purchaser himself. But if is not necessary to enter into that question, because the contract of sale is only alleged by way of inducement, the cause of action being, not upon that contract, but for an injury caused to the wife of the purchaser by reason of an article being sold to him for the use of his wife, and so sold to the defendant's knowledge, turning out to be unfit for the purpose for which it was bought. There is, therefore, no question of warranty to be considered, but whether the defendant, a chemist, compounding the article sold for a particular purpose, and knowing of the purpose for which it was bought, is liable in an action on the case for unskilfulness and negligence in the manufacture of it whereby the person who used it was injured. And I think that, quite apart from any question of warranty, express or implied, *there was a duty on the defendant, the vendor, to use ordinary care in compounding this wash for the hair.*

Unquestionably there was such a duty towards the purchaser, and it extends, in my judgment, to the person for whose use the vendor knew the compound was purchased." [Emphasis added.]

The reasoning in *George v Skivington* was taken a step further in *Heaven v Pender (1883) 11 Q.B.D. 503*. It is considered to be a case of first importance in the modern law of negligence. It appears to be the first ever case in which a serious attempt was made to establish a universally applicable test to determine whether a duty of care is owed by a defendant to a plaintiff. The facts were these.

The plaintiff was a workman employed by one Gray, a ship painter. The defendant was the owner of a dock. There was a ship at the dock that required painting. Gray contracted with the shipowner to paint the outside of the ship. The defendant, pursuant to the contract he had with the shipowner supplied a stage that was to be slung outside the ship. The stage was to be used by the plaintiff to paint the ship. It was within the defendant's contemplation that someone in the plaintiff's position would use the stage. The ropes by which the stage was slung were also supplied by the defendant. These ropes were unsafe for use, a fact which was discoverable through reasonably careful examination. When the plaintiff began to use the stage the ropes broke, the stage fell, and the plaintiff was injured. He sued the defendant in the tort of negligence. The Court of Appeal held for the plaintiff. Brett MR said:

"The proposition will stand thus: *whenever one person supplies goods, or machinery,*

> *or the like, for the purpose of their being used by another person under such circumstances that every one of ordinary sense would, if he thought, recognise at once that unless he used ordinary care and skill with regard to the condition of the thing supplied or the mode of supplying it, there will be danger of injury to the person or property of him for whose use the thing is supplied, and who is to use it, a duty arises to use ordinary care and skill as to the condition or manner of supplying such thing*. And for a neglect of such ordinary care or skill whereby injury happens a legal liability arises to be enforced by an action for negligence." [Emphasis added.]

You can see the introduction of a formula for product liability. A manufacturer must have in his contemplation those persons who will use his product. Hence, he must exercise reasonable care in manufacturing his product so that it will not cause harm to the users.

The next incremental move was in fact a giant step. It revolutionised the way lawyers thought. Its effects are still reverberating throughout the Commonwealth. It is a case every law student is familiar with. It is called *Donoghue v Stevenson [1932] AC 562*. It is a Scottish case. The facts are notorious. Here they are as stated in the pursuer's (the Scottish word for plaintiff) pleaded case.

The pursuer's friend bought her a bottle of ginger-beer which had been manufactured by the defendant. It was purchased from a retailer. The pursuer alleged that after she had drunk a substantial part of the contents, she found the bottle to contain the decomposed remains of a snail. She alleged that she suffered from shock and severe gastro-enteritis. She accordingly instituted the proceedings against the manufacturer. I must say something about the case which is of significance. In this case there was no trial. What the defender (the Scottish term for defendant) did was to say that even if all the facts pleaded by the pursuer were true he was nevertheless not liable. It was therefore only a point of law that was argued before the courts. It was never decided by any court that there was a snail in the bottle. The case was eventually settled. So, until today we do not even know if there really was a snail in that bottle.

The main arguments in the case were directed at the question whether the manufacturer of a product is liable in negligence to the ultimate consumer. But there was also an issue about the formulation of a general test for imposing a duty of care in general terms. When delivering the leading speech in the House of Lords was delivered by Lord Atkin. This is what he said:

> "It is remarkable how difficult it is to find in the English authorities statements of general application defining the relations between parties that give rise to the duty. The Courts are concerned with the particular relations which come before them in actual litigation, and it is sufficient to say whether the duty exists in those circumstances. The result is that the Courts have been engaged upon an elaborate

classification of duties as they exist in respect of property, whether real or personal, with further divisions as to ownership, occupation or control, and distinctions based on the particular relations of the one side or the other, whether manufacturer, salesman or landlord, customer, tenant, stranger, and so on."

He then went on to state the test as follows:

"At present I content myself with pointing out that in English law there must be, and is, some general conception of relations giving rise to a duty of care, of which the particular cases found in the books are but instances. The liability for negligence, whether you style it such or treat it as in other systems as a species of "culpa," is no doubt based upon a general public sentiment of moral wrongdoing for which the offender must pay. But acts or omissions which any moral code would censure cannot in a practical world be treated so as to give a right to every person injured by them to demand relief. In this way rules of law arise which limit the range of complainants and the extent of their remedy. *The rule that you are to love your neighbour becomes in law, you must not injure your neighbour; and the lawyer's question, Who is my neighbour? receives a restricted reply. You must take reasonable care to avoid acts or omissions*

> *which you can reasonably foresee would be likely to injure your neighbour. Who, then, in law is my neighbour? The answer seems to be - persons who are so closely and directly affected by my act that I ought reasonably to have them in contemplation as being so affected when I am directing my mind to the acts or omissions which are called in question.* This appears to me to be the doctrine of *Heaven v. Pender*." [Emphasis added.]

This passage has been and continues to be applied on countless occasions by courts throughout the Commonwealth.

As may be seen, it took the courts almost a hundred years to accept that the manufacturer owes a duty to the ultimate consumer of his product. It is only just that this be so. It is therefore clear that the coachman, Mr Winterbottom, ought to have succeeded. This is the negative aspect of the common law. It progresses very slowly and in the process does not produce a just result when it should.

Lecture 3

THE CONTINUUM OF LEGAL RESEARCH

1. PRIMARY SOURCES

In essence, legal research in the common law system has not changed for the last 250 years. The primary source of information for practitioners and judges continues to be textbooks. When a problem arises, the tendency for us is to go straight to one of the leading textbooks on the particular subject. And they are all available only in hard copies. Let me give you two instances from my own experience.

The first is a commercial case. We in the Court of Appeal had to determine whether the relationship between a bank and its customer had had superimposed on it a special relationship of joint venturers. To make that determination it was necessary for us to ascertain the meaning of a joint venture. And for that we turned to a renowned American textbook on the law of contracts called *Williston on Contracts*, 3rd ed. (1959). The next step in the case was to see if the law permits a court to infer a joint venture from a given set of facts. For this I turned to the analogy of a partnership. The first step in the legal research was to look at *Lindley on Partnership* which is a leading English work on the subject. But it provided no assistance. So, I turned up *SD Singh Gupta on the Law of Partnership*, and there I found two cases which said that a partnership can be inferred from an objective fact pattern. These are *Mirzamal Bhagwan Das v Rameshwar AIR 1929 All 536* and *Jakiuddin v Vithoba AIR 1939 Nag. 301*. I then went to the Manupatra online search engine and fed these two cases to see if they had been referred to in later cases. I found 4 cases which had referred to *Jakiuddin v Vithoba*. One of these, namely, *Meenakshi Achi v P.S.M. Subramanian Chettiar* which is an unreported case decided in 1956 was helpful. There, a Bench of the Madras High Court comprising Govinda Menon and Ramaswami, JJ said this:

> "In addition, a new partnership may be by an oral agreement or in writing. Again, it may be express or implied. It need not be express and can arise out of mutual understanding evidenced by a consistent course of conduct and by express admission of the parties concerned. Tajammal Hussain v. Ahmad Ali, AIR 1937 Oudh 438 (F); In re K. Narasayya, *MANU/TN/0248/1953* (G); Jakiuddin v. Vithoba, AIR 1939 Nag 301 (H): Chotte Lal v. Raj Mal, AIR 1951 Nag 448 (I); Haji Isa Haji Noor Finn v. Saru Bai, AIR 1938 Nag 324(J). See Lindley p. 105."

Note that the judgment cites other cases, including *In re K Narasayya* which carries only a Manupatra citation which I have underlined for ease of reference. This means that that case is otherwise not reported anywhere except by Manupatra.

Next on the trail, I went to Lexis Nexis online and searched for any cases in the Commonwealth and discovered two Canadian cases. They are *Johnson v Murray [1951] 2 W.W.R.(NS) 447* and; *Steward v Donnelly [2001] 108 A.C.W.S. (3d) 715*. So, when I came to write my judgment, this is what I said:

> "True that there is no formal written joint venture agreement in this case. But I do not regard that as being an impediment. In my judgment it is open to a court on an objective assessment of the proved and admitted facts to conclude that the true relationship between litigating parties was a joint venture. Just as a partnership may be implied by the conduct of parties (see, *Mirzamal Bhagwan Das v Rameshwar AIR* [1929] All 536 ; *Jakiuddin v Vithoba AIR* [1939] Nag. 301 ; *Johnson v Murray* [1951] 2 W.W.R.(NS) 447 at 448 ; *Steward v Donnelly* [2001] 108 A.C.W.S. (3d) 715) , so too may a joint venture."

The second instance is a case on administrative law. It concerned a company called Danaharta, which was created by statute and having extraordinary powers. The Government was the sole shareholder of the company. The question arose whether the company was subject to judicial review. The provision in the Malaysian Courts of Judicature Act 1964 conferring the power of judicial power in the High Court is very similar to Article 226 of the Indian Constitution. So, when dealing with the question at hand, we went straight to the leading textbooks on Indian Constitutional law and Administrative law and looked up decisions of the Indian Supreme Court which we later applied in our judgment. Among the texts we resorted to were Seervai's *Constitutional Law of India*, *Indian Constitutional Law* by MP Jain and Chaudhary on the Law of Writs. And this is what I said about the point at issue when delivering the majority judgment:

> "In the present instance, Danaharta, though a company incorporated under the Companies Act 1965 is wholly financed by public funds. Second, the affairs of Danaharta are directly or indirectly under the control of the Minister of Finance, representing the Federal Government. Third, the powers of Danaharta are, apart from its Memorandum of Association, conferred upon it by statute, *viz.*, the Danaharta Act. In these circumstances, and based on the authorities already cited, it is my considered judgment that Danaharta is a 'person or authority' within paragraph 1 and it is accordingly amenable to judicial review. In arriving at this conclusion, I have relied primarily on decisions of the Indian Supreme Court and not on English cases. This is because, our written law which governs a case of this nature, namely paragraph 1, has no parallel in England. When our Parliament deliberately puts on a course in public law that bears no resemblance to the English law of prerogative remedies, it would be wrong

for us as judges to change course."

In the sphere of legal research speed and convenience are often of the essence. It is therefore more expeditious and convenient if we are able to have a single text and a single book of cases covering all the various topics and sub-topics of the law. This has been provided for by two leading British works. The first is Halsbury's *Laws of England* and the second is the *Digest*, which was formerly called the *English and Empire Digest*.

Halsbury's *Laws of England* is a definitive encyclopedic treatise on the laws of England. It includes every proposition of English law (whether statutory or common law), with restatements of the common law and remarks to the relevant judicial authority and the statutory law which has in many cases codified, modified or supplemented common law. It is divided into alphabetically arranged titles, making it convenient to use and enabling quick and easy research into any area of law. It is named after Lord Halsbury, who was Lord Chancellor from 1885 to 1905 (with breaks in 1886 and 1892–1895). This is the longest tenure of a Lord Chancellor since Lord Eldon held that office in the early 19th century.

The first edition of this work commenced publication in 1907 and concluded in 1917. It comprises of 31 volumes and its editor-in-chief was the Earl of Halsbury himself. The second edition of Halsbury's *Laws of England* commenced publication in 1931 and was completed in 1942. It comes in 37 volumes with cumulative supplements. Its editor-in-chief was the then Lord Chancellor, Viscount Hailsham. The third edition commenced publication in 1952 and was completed in 1964. It comprises 43 volumes with cumulative supplements and its editor-in-chief was Viscount Simonds, the then Lord Chancellor.

It may be mentioned at this stage that all three editions are now out of print and are available only in leading law libraries. However, they are now readily available in microfiche form at William S. Hein & Co., Inc. of Buffalo, New York. The first edition is very useful and reliable not only for the purposes of ascertaining the law, but also as a starting point for obtaining cases and statutes in historical research.

Halsbury's 4th edition commenced publication in 1973 and is current with both periodical and cumulative supplements. The original editor-in-chief of the 4th edition was Lord Hailsham of St Marylebone but he has since passed away. Reissue volumes since August 1998 are published under the editorship of the Lord Mackay of Clashfern who was Lord Chancellor from 1987 to 1997. The text volumes are numbered 1 through 52. Volumes 53 to 56 are the Index volumes. The cumulative supplements are published annually and there is a *Current Service* in loose leaf form which is updated monthly.

Halsbury's *Laws of England* are now available on line but you have to subscribe for it. You have to go to the Edge Hill Home Page (http://www.edgehill.ac.uk) and choose Learning Services. A password is necessary to gain access.

Halsbury's *Laws* as a commentary are no longer confined to England. They have been extended to other countries under the auspices of Lexis Nexis which has done and continues to do sterling service for the legal profession. As presently advised, there is a Halsbury's *Laws of Australia*, of *India*, of *Hong Kong*, of *Malaysia* and *New Zealand*. The advantage of Halsbury's is that it is a textbook on every subject. Mention may here be made that the Halsbury's *Laws of Australia* are also available online.

As for a ready reference for cases, there are a number of English digests, but the most useful and comprehensive is *The English and Empire Digest*, which after 1981 came to be titled as *The Digest*. It covers cases from the Yearbooks to the present. Cases are arranged in classified sequence under broad subject headings and then chronologically within each topic. Each case is assigned a number that can be used to trace the later treatment of that case. This permits *The Digest* to be used as a citator. The cases are set out by name and citation. The Digest is organized along the lines of Halsbury's Laws of England Each volume has its own index and there is a two-volume general index of subjects and of words and phrases. The first edition of the English and Empire Digest was published from 1919 to 1932. The second or "Blue Band" edition was published from 1950 to 1970, and the third, or "Green Band", edition started in 1971 and continues with a rolling programme of re-issued volumes to bring the case law up to date. In some instances an older case may not be in the current digest and so resort to the older editions may be necessary. You may find it by checking one of the older editions. If the legal researcher knows only the name of a case, the Digest has Tables of Cases volumes which allow the researcher to find a case by name. They refer to the correct volume of The Digest which will then give the full citation for the case. The other advantage of the older editions is that they have a section at the end of each sub-topic that sets out decisions of other Commonwealth courts. This is extremely useful for practitioners and judges who wish to see how the same point has been dealt with in other jurisdictions.

In Canada, the *Canadian Abridgment* or *The Abridgment* is the most comprehensive research tool for Canadian law. *The Abridgment* may be used for several steps of the research process including locating case law and legislation, determining the judicial treatment of cases and legislation and also finding secondary sources. Generally the Abridgment is most useful once the researcher has already obtained a general overview of the research problem and is ready to look for more specific cases and legislation in the area. *The Abridgment* is divided into many components. These include the *Canadian Abridgment Case Digests* (CCD) which are published in more than 100 volumes. They are quite complicated and a little difficult to master. They are available online through the Westlaw e CARSWELL website. Practitioners and judges have to pay to gain access. The online *Abridgment* covers virtually every case recently reported in Canada, with the exception of Quebec civil law cases. It also includes every Court of Appeal case, whether reported or not, since 1987, every superior court case since 1996 and all other court cases since the end of 1998. CCD is available on CD-ROM (Folioviews). It is understood that the CD-ROM may be discontinued in future years, depending upon the success of the online version.

As for Australia, there is the *Australian Case Citator* which is useful if the researcher does not have the citation or requires as alternative citation. There is also the *Australian Digest* which comes in loose leaf binding. It provides digests or summaries of cases, and includes citation details. It commences coverage in the early 19th century and is continually updated. It is available both in hard copy and electronically. There is also another source called *Casebase* which is available electronically through Butterworths Online. Once you find a case in the Case Digests that interests you, you can link directly to the full text of the case without referring to a print copy.

As for India there are numerous hard copy publications of home grown commentaries and case digests. The ones that are most frequently used in Malaysia are *All India Reporter Commentaries on the Penal Code* and the *Criminal Procedure Code*, both of which are quite out of date and out of print. The two other works are the All India Reporter's *Criminal Digest* which is also out of date. The only commentary that is in current popular use in Malaysia is the *All India Reporter Manual*. The full set of the 5th edition and the first five volumes of the 6th edition of this work are available. The *Manual* is a section by section commentary of Indian Statutes arranged alphabetically. The advantage of the work is that it comprises of all the case law on each statute. One disadvantage of this work is that it is only the citation of a particular case that appears but not the name of the case. The other disadvantage is that the *Manual* does not contain a commentary of non-statutory case law. This need was at one time met by the *Quinquennial Digest* which came out in two editions both of which are now out of print. As India has a wealth of leading specialist textbooks on every subject (for example, Ejaz Ahmad on Criminal Breach of Trust) the *Digests* are hardly missed.

In Malaysia, at one time, in the field of commercial and company law we relied solely on English texts. That has now changed. We now primarily rely on Commonwealth texts. Unlike India, reliance on United States jurisprudence, even in the sphere of constitutional law is rare. A great majority of Malaysian statutes are in terms either identical or fairly similar to their Indian equivalent. So, it is quite common to find our courts referring to leading Indian texts such as Sohoni's *Commentaries on the Criminal Procedure Code*, Sir Hari Singh Gour's work on the Indian Penal Code and Sarkar or Woodroffe & Ameerali on the Law of Evidence, Ramaiya's *Company Law*, Pollock & Mulla's work on the Indian Contract Act of 1872 and Dr Banerjee's work or Anand & Iyer's work on the Indian Specific Relief Act. We also refer to works from Canada, Australia, New Zealand South Africa and the Caribbean.

In recent times we have produced our own authors some of whose work is up to international standards. Malaysian authors unlike their counterparts in other countries have the unenviable task of finding out the treatment rendered by courts of several Commonwealth countries on a given topic. They then have to discuss and notate cases from several jurisdictions on that topic. As such, Malaysian texts are far more useful to a practitioner or a judge in, say, India or Australia as they inform their readers what the law is across the Commonwealth.

2. GETTING TO THE CASES

Hard copies of law reports are still the preferred source of case law research. In recent times the number of law reports has increased in geometric proportions. There are literally hundreds of volumes that are produced each year. Some of them are generic; like the *All England Law Reports*, the *Commonwealth Law Reports* (from Australia), the *Dominion Law Reports* from Canada and the *All India Reporter*. There are also State reports in Australia, India and the United States and Provincial reports from Canada.

Again there are specialist reports like the *Building* Law Reports, the Construction Law Reports, the Commercial Law Reports and Personal Injury and Quantum Reports. Added to this is the fact that the same case may be reported in more than one report. Take the case of *Wiszniewski v Central Manchester Health Authority* which is a case on medical negligence. It is reported in [1998] P.I.Q.R. 324 and also in [1998] Lloyd's Rep. Med. 223, both of which are specialist reports. So, if you practice medical negligence, you will need these specialist reports in addition to the other generic law reports. But there is an added feature about this case. It discusses well an important point of civil procedure that is vital to a practitioner at the commercial Bar. So, if you are such a practitioner, you too will need this report. This state of affairs creates two major problems: first as to space and second as to expense.

Storage space is a major problem for lawyers and law libraries. With a constantly expanding library one has to keep expanding the area under occupation.

The larger the area, the greater the maintenance that is required. As some of the law reports are very old, the paper on which they are printed have, in the course of time become brittle. Even with the use of extreme care may result in pages being permanently damaged. Those familiar with some of the older Indian reports such as the *Calcutta Weekly* Notes and the older *Indian Law Reports* will be able to testify to this fact.

The second and more important issue is finance. The cost of printing has increased substantially in the last 25 years. Even standard English texts have become cost prohibitive. For example, Lindley on Partnership costs about US$500 per copy. So too, law reports have become very expensive to acquire. And once acquired, you must subscribe for current issues, unless it is a series that is no longer in publication, like the Indian Cases, the *Calcutta Weekly Notes* or the first series of the *Dominion Law Reports*.

The long term answer to these problems is electronic sourcing of information, particularly the decided cases. And that is, I think, the way of things to come.

3. THE WAY FORWARD

Currently there are at least five online databases that contain information sought by the members of the legal profession. They are Lexis Nexis, Westlaw, Justis, Manupatra, the *Malaysian Current Law Journal*, the Her Majesty's Court Service, the House of Lords website, the Privy Council website (which has a hyperlink to the judgments of the Privy Council), the Judgment Information System (JUDIS) in India and the World Legal Information Institute (WORLDLII). In addition, there are the *South African Law Reports*, the *English Reports*, the *AIR Supreme Court Cases* from 1950 to 2005 and the *Malayan Law Journal* which are available on CD ROM.

Of all the online electronic databases, the last five are available without payment. All the others are only available through subscription. And some of the subscription charges are quite expensive. For example, the subscription to Justis for two services, namely, the *English Reports* and the *Irish Reports* costs a little more than US$1000 per year.

The problem relating to the access to judgments has been neatly put by Lord Justice Brooke in his paper titled "Publishing the Courts: Judgments and Public Information on the Internet" presented at the 13th Commonwealth Law Conference, 2003:

> "Why have I always been so enthusiastic about the need for free provision for primary sources of legal information? My answer is that I have always been keen to establish a level playing-field in access to the law. Our great long-established universities have always had wonderful law libraries. So have the Inns of Court and the Advocates' Library in Edinburgh and our leading lawyers' offices in this island and their equivalents in Belfast and Dublin.
>
> But what about the universities which started developing law faculties from 1960 onwards? What about the smaller lawyers' offices, particularly those away from big urban centres? What about the courts

themselves, particularly the smaller courts, and the judges and magistrates and sheriffs who sit there? What about law centres and *pro bono* units and citizens' advice bureaux? What about the countries of the Commonwealth, particularly in Africa and the Caribbean, which are desperate to obtain access to UK law texts?

The world I watched developing in the 1990s was a world in which the gap between the haves and the have-nots was widening. As the courts provided more and more of their judgments in written form, the lawyers involved in the cases had the precious transcripts photocopied or scanned onto their firm's or their chambers' or their offices' electronic databases, available only to a comparatively small circle. Electronic publishers got hold of these unpublished court transcripts and created subscription services for the customers who could afford to pay for them. Unless there was a brief summary in a newspaper law report, the rest of the market was left to wait for the report eventually to be published in one of the series of law reports to which they had access. Often they had to wait a long time.

More and more specialist law report series were also being created, and there was a limit to the number of law reports most people practising or studying or teaching the law could afford."

So it comes to this. Textbooks, law reports, both hard copies and online are almost always cost prohibitive. How then does the not so well to do lawyer gain access to information that he so vitally needs to advise his client and to earn a decent living for himself? The answer is for the courts, either acting on their own or together with universities, to make law reports available for free on the Internet.

A step in this direction was taken in Australia, when, several years ago when a search engine called "Sinosearch" was launched as a website. It gave free access to cases decided by the courts of Australia. This was overreached by AustLII which was the pioneering work of two Australian universities. AustLII was founded on the principle that everyone should have access to both the written law and the case law of their country free of charge. If you log in to the AustLII website, you will have immediate free access to a database that has many statutes and judgments not only of the courts in Australia but also to important tribunals jurisdictions. They have a complex software by which fresh material can be uploaded and integrated into their database through an automatic process.

There then followed the establishment of Legal Information Institutes in several common law countries, including the United States whose participation is through Cornell University. On 3 October 2002 the meeting of the various Legal Informartion Institutes (LIIs) in Montreal at the 4th Law via Internet Conference, made a declaration as a joint statement of their philosophy of access to law. There were some further modifications of the

Declaration at the Sydney meeting of LIIs in 2003 and at the Paris meeting in 2004. The Montreal Declaration reads as follows:

> "Public legal information from all countries and international institutions is part of the common heritage of humanity. Maximising access to this information promotes justice and the rule of law;

* Public legal information is digital common property and should be accessible to all on a non-profit basis and free of charge;
* Independent non-profit organisations have the right to publish public legal information and the government bodies that create or control that information should provide access to it so that it can be published.

Public legal information means legal information produced by public bodies that have a duty to produce law and make it public. It includes primary sources of law, such as legislation, case law and treaties, as well as various secondary (interpretative) public sources, such as reports on preparatory work and law reform, and resulting from boards of inquiry. It also includes legal documents created as a result of public funding.

A legal information institute:

* Publishes via the internet public legal information originating from more than one public body;
* Provides free, full and anonymous public access to that information;
* Does not impede others from publishing public legal information; and

* Supports the objectives set out in this Declaration.

All legal information institutes are encouraged to participate in regional or global free access to law networks.

Therefore, the legal information institutes agree:

* To promote and support free access to public legal information throughout the world, principally via the Internet;
* To cooperate in order to achieve these goals and, in particular, to assist organisations in developing countries to achieve these goals, recognising the reciprocal advantages that all obtain from access to each other's law;
* To help each other and to support, within their means, other organisations that share these goals with respect to:
  - Promotion, to governments and other organisations, of public policy conducive to the accessibility of public legal information;
  - Technical assistance, advice and training;
  - Development of open technical standards; and
  - Academic exchange of research results.
* To meet at least annually, and to invite other organisations who are legal information institutes to subscribe to this declaration and join those meetings, according to procedures to be established by the parties to this Declaration.
* To provide to the end users of public legal

information clear information concerning any conditions of re-use of that information, where this is feasible.

The parties to the Montreal Declaration were the Australasian Legal Information Institute, the British and Irish Legal Information Institute, the LexUM/ Canadian Legal Information Institute, the Hong Kong Legal Information Institute, the Legal Information Institute (Cornell), the Pacific Islands Legal Information Institute, the University of the West Indies Faculty of Law Library, and Wits University School of Law (South Africa).

WORLDLII now carries hyperlinks to the various Legal Information Institutes. Free access to the judgments of the courts of the participating countries is available. In September 2005, on the sidelines of the Commonwealth Law Conference was launched the Commonwealth Legal Information Institute or COMLII which is hyperlinked to 469 databases from 52 Commonwealth and common law countries and territories in collaboration with members of the Free Access to Law Movement.

The obvious advantage of COMLII is that access to the most recent judgments and some of the older ones is absolutely free. There is however no value added material and all that is available are the raw judgments. But many may not see this as a disadvantage because lawyers are by their training quite used to reading judgments in full for the purpose of either applying or distinguishing them. The other problem with COMLII is that there is a timeline limit on availability. Some of the older cases are not as yet available. But it must be said at once that in the case of Australia, all the reports of their High Court are available from 1903 when they first went into print. Also, serious efforts are being made to upload the earlier cases from other jurisdictions as well. For example, CANLII which only had decisions of the Canadian Supreme Court from 1985, has now uploaded and made available cases from 1974 to 2006. A total of 4,629 decisions of the Supreme Court are available on the CANLII database. Of these 2,315 are in English and 2,314 are in French. At present CanLII generally publishes decisions within 24 to 48 hours following public availability.

In India there are two online research databases. One is JUDIS which is managed by the Courts Informatics Division of the National Informatics Centre of the Ministry of Information Technology. Access is completely free of charge. The website has decisions of the Supreme Court and nine High Courts. The search engine for High Courts is limited to four search terms, namely, the name of the party (petitioner or respondent), the case number, the judge's name and text or phrase. Not all judgments of all the courts are available at the website. For example, in the case of the Madras High Court, cases decided between 1999 and 2006 are available. In the case of the Supreme Court, an additional two search terms are available, namely, Act of Parliament and headnote. Supreme Court decisions from 1977 are available. The other online server is Manupatra which is particularly user-friendly. It has all the cases decided by the Supreme Court and most of the cases decided by the High Courts of India from 1950. However, in the case of the Bombay High Court the decisions available online go back to 1903. This is useful because the reports include cases decided by the Privy Council on appeal from the Bombay High Court. It would be extremely useful to us in Malaysia - and I am sure other Commonwealth jurisdictions - if the pre-1950 cases from all Indian High Courts as well as the decisions of the Privy Council in respect of appeals from India are made available online.

In Malaysia, we rely on Lexis Nexis and the *Malaysian Current Law Journal* for online information support. Both these services are only available on payment. The advantage of Lexis Nexis which is used in many countries is that it makes available online cases and materials (including statutes) from several jurisdictions. At present, case law from 23 sources is available. This includes the United States, the Commonwealth (excluding the East and West African countries and the Pacific Islands), the South African Constitutional cases and Hong Kong. If you know the name of a case and want to find out if it has been referred to or applied in any of the available sources, all you have to do is to click on "case analysis", type in the name of the case and click on the search button. The system will then throw up all the cases decided in any of the jurisdictions on the Lexis Nexis database which have referred to the case in question. Lexis Nexis is engineered in such a way that you can leave it on without using it for howsoever long a period without the system shutting down or the search expiring. In the case of Malaysian cases, every judgment received by Lexis is uploaded in raw form onto the system within 24 hours of receipt of the judgment and is available under the list of *Malayan Law Journal Unreported Cases*. These are some of the advantages of Lexis. The downside is that not all the cases decided by the English Courts are available on Lexis Nexis. This holds especially true for some of the specialist reports. But I have found the advantages far outweigh the disadvantages. Lexis Nexis also makes available on CD ROM cases decided by Malaysian and Singaporean Courts from 1932 up to date. The CD is updated from time to time and also has a section on articles published in the *Malayan Law Journal* from time to time.

The *Malaysian Current Law Journal* (CLJ) website has cases decided by Malaysian Courts since 1997. This also has a user friendly search engine. It is however limited to Malaysian cases. One advantage is that that some judgments not reported by the *Malayan Law Journal* are available on the CLJ website. The other advantage is that the home page carries two of the most recent and objectively important decisions of the Malaysian Courts.

The third electronic source we rely on in Malaysia is Westlaw International which is also a service only available on payment. It is available in other countries as well. Its database carries cases and materials from the Commonwealth (except the African jurisdictions and the Pacific Islands). Cases not available on other databases (such as Lexis) are available on Westlaw. Access to Canadian, Hong Kong and UK statutes and regulations may also be had. Further, the *Melbourne Law Review* (only from 1997), the *Singapore Journal of International and Comparative Law*, the *Hong Kong Law Journal* (only from 2001) and UK law journals legal periodicals and reviews published by Swet & Maxwell and Oxford University Press may be accessed. This facility is not available on Lexis. But the Westlaw system has three very serious downsides. First it is not as user-friendly as Lexis. Second, it does not have any Indian, Malaysian, Singapore and South African cases. Third, the length of search time is seriously limited. If the system is left unused for a short while it logs off automatically and you have to log in afresh. This has an adverse effect on a search trail that the researcher may be working on Lexis does not have this problem.

4. STRIKING A BALANCE

If everyone concerned in the justice process – counsel for all the parties and the court – are fully armed with all the relevant authorities, the chances of arriving at a just decision are better. For, justice in court proceedings is in accordance with the law and not in some abstract sense.

In the ordinary way, courts look to advocates for assistance in arriving at a right and just decision. To be able to provide that assistance there must be a ready source of information available across the board. Otherwise, only the rich and powerful will be armed with upto date information and the poor and weak will not. "The poor" of course includes advocates who are under financial constraint to have access to developments throughout the common law world. This is what Lord Justice Brooke (in the passage already quoted) was referring to as "a level playing field". Issues of copyright, however, prevent – and quite rightly so – the reproduction of original work without the consent of the true owner of the work. In the case of law reports this covers the editing of a judgment through value-added material such as the headnote to a case or an editorial note to the case.

But the raw judgment itself is *publici juris* or public property and carries no rights to copyright in anyone. So, the reproduction of raw judgments on the Internet is not a breach of copyright.

Accessibility free of cost to the wealth of common law jurisprudence is one factor that will ensure a level playing field. The other is a genuine earnestness on the part of lawyers, judges and academics to research a point to see how other jurisdictions have dealt with it. An absence of this drive for acquiring knowledge will lead to the frog in a well syndrome which is symptomatic of a contentedness on the part of the legal profession in each common law jurisdiction to looking just at the decisions of their domestic courts without caring what is happening in other countries.

As for the courts, by being supplied with up to date information, we are less likely to get a point of law wrong. You can well imagine the difficulties that will ensue if different Benches of our courts make decisions in ignorance of recent judgments on the same point decided either by another Bench or by a court in another common law jurisdiction. Before the era of the electronic information explosion, we had to wait for several weeks to be made aware of a decision of the courts of the Commonwealth. The only information that was available in a fairly short time was the airmail version of the *Times Law Report*. This was very expensive and some of us have discontinued using it for that reason as well as for the reason that the same information is now available free on Bailii. Today the story is quite different. Judgments are available free of charge within hours of their being handed down.

In Malaysia we do have a website for our courts on which judgments of our superior courts are posted. Judgments are posted within 24 hours of their receipt by the Information Technology Department of the courts. Any delay is usually caused by the failure of the secretaries of individual judges to send in judgments to the Information Technology Department. As a result there is some delay in the posting of judgments. Consequently the information is not always up to date. This hampers both advocates as well as the courts at all levels.

The downside of free access to electronic judgments is that there is a risk of a surfeit of paper descending on the Bench either during oral argument or by way of written submissions. Counsel sometimes have the tendency of citing decisions on facts as supporting a legal proposition. As one of our judges, Mahadev Shankar said in the case of *Public Prosecutor v Kang Ho Soh [1992] 1 MLJ 360*, about the citation of authorities on an issue that was plainly one of fact:

> "With respect to the industry of counsel and the Deputy Public Prosecutor I feel I ought to say something here about the system of judicial precedent. That statements made by an accused person after his arrest are inadmissible, unless the statutory preconditions laid down by s 37A of the [Dangerous Drugs] Act are satisfied, is of course a matter of law. But whether in a particular case a person was under actual arrest at a given moment in time is a question of fact, to be decided according to the circumstances of each case. It is well

> established that the reasons given by a judge for arriving at a conclusion of fact, is not to be treated as law and therefore citable. Failure to appreciate this can result in the court being crushed under the weight of its own reports (see *Qualcast (Wolverhampton) Ltd v Haynes* [1959] AC 743, at pp 757, 758, 759 and 761.)"

In other words, counsel cite cases which do not decide any new point of law but which merely illustrate the application of well established principles of law to a new set of facts.

So how do we strike a balance?

In England, the courts have tried to hold a balance by issuing Practice Direction (Citation of Authorities) [2001] 1 WLR 1001; [2001] 2 All ER 510. One of the things that this does is to prohibit the citation by advocates of judgments on applications for permission to appeal unless they clearly indicate that they purport to establish a new principle or to extend the present law. But it has not really helped. As Lord Justice Brooke says: "Very often lawyers can't recognise a principle of law when they see one. We are getting steadily more and more overloaded with citations of cases which frequently don't help us in the task we have got to do but which just add to the paper we have to read." It would appear that my learned brother of the English Court of Appeal is merely echoing the views of judges in many jurisdictions.

It follows that the better of the two evils seems to be to allow counsel access to as much law as possible hoping that they will cite only relevant cases. And when they do not, the burden will fall on us, the judges, to sift the wheat from the chaff.

Appendix-2

Academic Writings That Influenced Decisions

EXAMPLE I

1. In 1981, the UK Parliament passed the Criminal Attempts Act. Section 1 (2) of the Act provides that:-

   "A person may be guilty of attempting to commit an offence to which this section applies even though the facts are such that the commission of the offence is impossible."

   In *Anderton v Ryan [1985] AC 567*, the accused handled a video recorder in the belief that it was stolen when it was not. The House of Lords held that where a person dishonestly handled goods in the belief that they were stolen when in fact they were not stolen he was not guilty of attempting dishonestly to handle stolen goods.

2. Following this decision, Professor Glanville Williams wrote an article in which he severely criticised the House of Lords. Shortly after *Anderton's case*, the case of *R v Shivpuri [1986]*

2 All ER 334 came before the House of Lords. It was now acknowledged by the court that the decision in *Anderton's case* was wrong. In the course of his speech, Lord Bridge said this:

> "I cannot conclude this opinion without disclosing that I have had the advantage, since the conclusion of the argument in this appeal, of reading an article by Professor Glanville Williams entitled "The Lords and Impossible Attempts, or Quis Custodiet Ipsos Custodes?" [1986] C.L.J. 33. The language in which he criticises the decision in Anderton v. Ryan is not conspicuous for its moderation, but it would be foolish, on that account, not to recognise the force of the criticism and churlish not to acknowledge the assistance I have derived from it."

EXAMPLE II

3. Sometimes two authors may present opposite views and the court may prefer the one to the other.

4. In *Westdeutsche Landesbank Girozentrale v. Islington London Borough Council [1996] AC 669*, the House of Lords was faced with the issue whether a resulting trust should be held to arise whenever money is paid under a mistake. There were two conflicting views by two academics, both from Oxford University. The first was the late Professor Birks who argued that a resulting trust does arise in such circumstances. However, William Swadling argued otherwise. This is what

Lord Browne-Wilkinson said about it:

"It is true that the parties were under a misapprehension that the payment was made in pursuance of a valid contract. But that does not alter the actual intentions of the parties at the date the payment was made or the moneys were mixed in the bank account. As the article by William Swadling, "A new role for resulting trusts?" 16 Legal Studies 133 demonstrates the presumption of resulting trust is rebutted by evidence of any intention inconsistent with such a trust, not only by evidence of an intention to make a gift.

Professor Birks, "Restitution and Resulting Trusts" (see Equity: Contemporary Legal Developments, p. 335, at p. 360) ...suggests that a resulting trust should arise wherever the money is paid under a mistake (because such mistake vitiates the actual intention) or when money is paid on a condition which is not subsequently satisfied. As one would expect, the argument is tightly reasoned but I am not persuaded."

...

If adopted, Professor Birks's wider concepts would give rise to all the practical consequences and injustices to which I have referred."

EXAMPLE III

5. Writings of academics have also influenced decisions of courts in the field of constitutional law.

6. Until very recently, lawyers thought that Dicey's Rule of Law was confined to only the procedural arena of public law. It has been said on many occasions that substance and procedure are to be kept apart. An extreme position was taken was in *Gopalan v State of Madras AIR 1950 SC 27* where it was held that "law" in article 21 of the Indian Constitution meant only written law and did not include the rules of natural justice which are part and parcel of the Rule of Law. Let me quote from:

(i) Kania CJ:

> "The only right is that no person shall be deprived of his life or liberty except according to procedure established by law. One may like that right to cover a larger area, but to give such a right is not the function of the Court; it is the function of the Constitution. To read the word 'law' as meaning rules of natural justice will land one in difficulties because the rules of natural justice, as regards procedure, are nowhere defined and in my opinion the Constitution cannot be read as laying down a vague standard. It is obvious that in that clause 'law' must mean enacted law."

(ii) Patanjali Sastri J:

> "Giving full effect to these principles, however, I am unable to agree that the term "Law" in Art. 21 means the immutable and universal principles of natural justice. "Procedure established by law" must be taken to refer to a procedure which has a statutory origin, for no procedure is known or can be said to have been established by such vague and uncertain concepts as "the immutable and universal principles of natural justice". In my opinion, "law" in Art. 21 means "positive or State made law"."

(iii) Mukherjea J:

> "My conclusion, therefore, is that in Art. 21 the word 'law' has been used in the sense of State-made law and not as an equivalent of law in the abstract or general sense embodying the principles of natural justice. The Article presupposes that the law is a valid and binding law under the provisions of the Constitution having regard to the competency of the legislature and the subject it relates to and does not infringe any of the fundamental rights which the constitution provides for."

7. However, these views were exploded by Lord Diplock in *Ong Ah Chuan v Public Prosecutor [1981] 1 MLJ 64* where he said this in relation to the Singapore Constitution:

> "In a constitution founded on the Westminster model and particularly in that

part of it that purports to assure to all individual citizens the continued enjoyment of fundamental liberties or rights, references to 'law' in such context as 'in accordance with law', 'equality before the law', 'protection of the law' and the like, in their Lordships' view, refer to a system of law which incorporates those fundamental rules of natural justice that had formed part and parcel of the common law of England that was in operation in Singapore at the commencement of the Constitution. It would have been taken for granted by makers of the Constitution that the 'law' to which citizens could have recourse for the protection of fundamental liberties assured to them by the Constitution would be a system of law that did not flout those fundamental rules. If it were otherwise it would be misuse of language to speak of law as something which affords 'protection' for the individual in the enjoyment of his fundamental liberties, and the purported entrenchment (by article 5) of articles 9(1) and 12(1) would be little better than a mockery."

8. I now come to the critical authority. In *Pierson v Secretary of State for the Home Department [1997] 3 All ER 577, at p 606* Lord Steyn was influenced by the writings of learned academics to conclude that the Rule of Law had both procedural and substantive dimensions. He said:

"But counsel addressed the wrong target.

The correct analysis of this case is in terms of the rule of law. The rule of law in its wider sense has procedural and substantive effect. While Dicey's description of the rule of law (Introduction to the Study of the Law of the Constitution, 10th Ed., 1968; p 203) is nowadays regarded as neither exhaustive nor entirely accurate even for his own time, there is much of enduring value in the work of this great lawyer. Dicey's famous third meaning of the rule of law is apposite. He said:

'The "rule of law", lastly, may be used as a formula for expressing the fact that with us the law of constitution, the rules which in foreign countries naturally form part of a constitutional code, are not the source but the consequence of the rights of individuals, as defined and enforced by the courts; that, in short, the principles of private law have with us been by the action of the courts and Parliament so extended as to determine the position of the Crown and its servants; thus the constitution is the result of the ordinary law of the land.'

This was the pivot of Dicey's discussion of rights to personal freedom, and to freedom of association and of public meeting (see pp 206–283). It is clear therefore that in the relevant sense Dicey regarded the rule of law as having both procedural and substantive effect. In a valuable essay Professor Jeffrey Jowell has re-examined

Dicey's theme: see 'The Rule of Law Today' in The Changing Constitution by Jowell and Oliver, 3rd Ed., 1994; pp 74–77. Relying on striking modern illustrations, Professor Jowell concluded that the rule of law has substantive content: see Hall & Co Ltd v Shoreham-by-Sea UDC [1964] 1 All ER 1, [1964] 1 WLR 1240, Congreve v Home Office [1976] 1 All ER 697, [1976] QB 629 and Wheeler v Leicester City Council [1985] 2 All ER 1106, [1985] AC 1054 per Lord Templeman, with whom Lord Bridge of Harwich, Lord Brightman and Lord Griffiths agreed. Wade Administrative Law (7th Ed, 1994) pp 24ff and de Smith and Brazier Constitutional and Administrative Law,7th Ed., 1994; p 18, are to the same effect. Unless there is the clearest provision to the contrary, Parliament must be presumed not to legislate contrary to the rule of law. And the rule of law enforces minimum standards of fairness, both substantive and procedural. I therefore approach the problem in the present case on this basis."

8. Another illustration is in the area of the right of citizens to share in the benefits of development in a welfare State, including free or State subsidised education. Here the article of *Charles A. Reich titled "The New Property" in (1964) 73 Yale Law Journal, 733* has influenced the thinking of judges in at least two jurisdictions. You will find it referred to in United States cases of *Madera v Board of Education (1967) 267 F. Supp*

356, Hanley v Maine School Administrative District (Unreported, decided on June 29, 1979) and Andersen v Massachusetts Institute of Technology (1995) 3 Mass. L. Rep. 293.

9. In India, it has been quoted with approval in *Ramana Dayaram Shetty v. International Airport Authority of India AIR 1979 SC 1628*. In that case Bhagwati J said:

"The valuables dispensed by Government take many forms, but they all share one characteristic. They are steadily taking the place of traditional forms of wealth. These valuables which derive from relationships to Government are of many kinds. They comprise social security benefits, cash grants for political sufferers and the whole scheme of State and local welfare. Then again, thousands of people are employed in the State and the Central Government and local authorities. Licences are required before one can engage in many kinds of businesses or work. The power of giving licences means power to withhold them and this gives control to the Government or to the agents of Government on the lives of many people. Many individuals and many more businesses enjoy largess in the form of Government contracts. These contracts often resemble subsidies. It is virtually impossible to lose money on them and many enterprises are set up primarily to do business with Government. Government owns and controls hundreds of acres of public land valuable for mining, and other purposes. These resources are available for utilisation by private corporations and individuals by way of lease or licence. All these mean growth in the Government largess and with the increasing magnitude and range of governmental functions as we move closer to a welfare State, more and more of our wealth consists of these new forms. Some of these forms of wealth may be in the nature of legal rights but the large majority of them are in the nature of privileges. But on that account, can it be said that they do not enjoy any legal protection? Can they be regarded as gratuity furnished by the State so that the State may withhold, grant or revoke it at its pleasure? Is the position of the Government in this respect the same as that of a private giver? We do not think so. The law has not been slow to recognise the importance of this new kind of wealth and the need to protect individual interest in it and with that end in view, it has developed new forms of protection. Some interests in Government largess, formerly regarded as privileges, have been recognised as rights while others have been given legal protection not only by forging procedural safeguards but also by confining / structuring and checking Government discretion in the matter of grant of such largess. The discretion of the Government has been held to be not unlimited in that the Government cannot give or withhold largess in its arbitrary discretion or at its sweet will. It is insisted, as pointed out by Professor Reich in an especially stimulating article on *'The New Property'* in *73 Yale Law Journal 733*, 'that Government action be based on standards that are not arbitrary or unauthorised.' The Government cannot be permitted to say that it will give jobs or enter into contracts or issue quotas or licences only in favour of those having grey hair or belonging to a particular political party or professing a particular religious faith. The Government is still the Government when it acts in the matter of granting largess and it cannot act arbitrarily. It does not stand in the same position as a private individual."

10. In the light of the foregoing discussion, it is difficult to accept as universally correct the following view expressed by Professor Madison of the University of Pittsburgh in his article "*The Idea of the Law Review*":

"[J]udges often believe that law professors believe that law professors are more important than judges. Perhaps more than anything else, that explains the occasional burst of judicial hostility toward legal scholarship."

But it is impossible for us not to agree with his view that:

"[I]t's not much of an exaggeration to say

that a *Harvard Law Review* article did, indeed, create the law. Getting a *Harvard Law Review* article cited by the Supreme Court of the United States is the sort of thing that can go to your head. In fact, it may be just about the only thing that can briefly unsettle the belief that law professors are the most important members of the legal profession."

INDEX